POKER
FOR
WOMEN

POKER FOR WOMEN

A Course in Destroying Male Opponents
at Poker. . .and Beyond

By
Mike Caro

"The Mad Genius"

A GAMBLING TIMES BOOK

DISTRIBUTED BY
LYLE STUART
Secaucus, N.J.

POKER FOR WOMEN
Copyright ©1986 by Gambling Times Incorporated

ISBN: 0-89746-009-X

Distributed by Lyle Stuart, Inc.

Manufactured in the United States of America
First Printing—February 1986

Cover Design and Illustration: *Terry Robinson*

All material presented in this book is offered as information to the reader. No inducement to gamble is intended or implied.

OTHER BOOKS PUBLISHED BY GAMBLING TIMES

(See page 211 for details)

Poker Books

According to Doyle by Doyle Brunson
Caro On Gambling by Mike Caro
Caro's Book of Tells by Mike Caro
Free Money: How to Win in the Cardrooms of California by Michael Wiesenberg
How to Win at Poker Tournaments by Tom McEvoy
New Poker Games by Mike Caro
The Railbird by Rex Jones
Tales Out of Tulsa by Bobby Baldwin
Wins, Places and Pros by Tex Sheahan

Blackjack Books

The Beginner's Guide to Winning Blackjack by Stanley Roberts
The GT Guide to Blackjack by Stanley Roberts and others
Million Dollar Blackjack by Ken Uston
Winning Blackjack by Stanley Roberts

Casino Games

The GT Guide to Casino Games by Len Miller
The GT Guide to Craps by N.B. Winkless, Jr.

General Interest Books

The GT Guide to Gaming Around the World

The GT Guide to Systems That Win, Volumes I and II
The GT Guide to Winning Systems, Volumes I and II
GT Presents Winning Systems and Methods, Volumes I and II
The GT Quiz Book by Mike Caro
The Mathematics of Gambling by Dr. Edward O. Thorp
P$yching Out Vegas by Marvin Karlins, Ph.D.
Winning By Computer by Dr. Donald Sullivan

Sports Betting Books

Fast Track to Thoroughbred Profits by Mark Cramer
The GT Guide to Basketball Handicapping by Barbara Nathan
The GT Guide to Football Handicapping by Bob McCune
The GT Guide to Greyhound Racing by William E. McBride
The GT Guide to Harness Racing by Igor Kusyshyn, Ph.D., Al Stanley and Sam Dragich
The GT Guide to Jai Alai by William R. Keevers
The GT Guide to Thoroughbred Racing by R.G. Denis

Mike Caro, gambling's "Mad Genius."

About the Author

Mike Caro is today's leading authority on poker psychology, strategy and statistics. In his books, columns and seminars, he teaches a dynamic winning style that has earned him the title: "the Mad Genius of Poker."

For over five years, Caro has clarified and pioneered some of the most important gambling concepts ever put on paper. He is consultant to many of the world's leading poker players and his advice on casino games and gambling in general is highly regarded throughout the world.

Caro is primarily known as a teacher and theorist, but beyond that—twice world poker champion—Doyle Brunson, calls him "the best draw poker player alive."

The "Mad Genius" is a computer wizard who uses his exclusive programs to back up his research. His in-depth statistics on poker and gambling are among the most widely quoted today. In addition, he is famous for his work on the psychology and philosophy of gambling.

Mike Caro is Poker Editor of *Gambling Times* magazine and a columnist for *Poker Player* newspaper. Much of his writing is unconventional and very profound. Yet he explains things in crisp, clear language that will have your pulse racing as you learn the secret ways to winning. *Mike Caro's Book of Tells* after many years of research has just recently been published by Gambling Times Incorporated and is fast becoming a runaway best seller.

We think what you're about to read here in *Poker for Women* will surprise you. And if gambling is part of your nature (in poker *and* in the world beyond poker), this book might become one of your best friends for life.

TABLE OF CONTENTS

Introduction

Before you read this book, go ahead and ask me some questions.

1. *Should men read* Poker for Women? Definitely. They may discover how to guard themselves against devastating advanced tactics available only to females.

2. *Is this book directed to women?* Yes. When I use the word *you*, I will usually be thinking of my reader as a woman. Men may learn by following along, but they are not specifically addressed on these pages.

3. *Is this book exclusively about poker?* No, but poker provides a perfect playground for applying techniques that destroy male adversaries.

4. *Where can these methods be used away from the poker table?* Lots of places. There is a larger game beyond poker, and it is all around you. Even though those words may sound philosophical, they aren't intended to be. I am speaking now in a purely practical, scientific way; and I am saying that you exist in an environment that is very often analogous to a poker game. Once you understand poker science and how you can use tactics that turn male prejudices in your favor, you'll be able to employ these same winning tactics every day, even if you seldom sit in a poker game.

5. *Can poker be played for profit?* Sure. This book will train you to do it. There are already many women and men who earn their livings entirely by playing poker. Don't confuse poker with unbeatable games of chance such as craps, keno and roulette. Poker is a game of skill in which good players beat bad players.

6. *Where can poker be played legally?* There is legal public poker in California, Nevada, Washington, Oregon and Montana. Additionally, you may have the opportunity to earn money by play-

ing in home games or in semi-private games such as those at country clubs. The public card rooms are your best bet, because they cater to women customers. Private games sometimes bar women players, either overtly or tacitly.

7. *Isn't poker just another sick form of competition that keeps us from living in peace and cooperation?* I'm glad you asked that question. I'm familiar with those popular anti-competition books of a dozen years ago. Cooperation is just swell with me. But by competing, we can learn to function at more intense levels; we can acquire skills which would not be attainable if we weren't pushed to new levels by an opponent. Anyway, that's how I feel about it. If you still think you can succeed without "playing games," then do it. Hide this book on your shelf for a while. Perhaps we'll never meet again. Or, maybe, someday when you're getting outmaneuvered and battered about by someone who keeps right on playing games without your permission, you'll return to these pages. And I'll teach you how to win.

Chapter One

What is Poker, Anyway?

Sometimes I lie in bed and dream about all the futile things a human being can accomplish. One futile thing would be to write this book on the assumption that every reader knows how to play poker.

Besides being futile, that would be a great moral evil, because I've already promised that the principal values herein lie beyond poker. Since this book doesn't confine itself to the narrow arena of cards, but rather uses winning poker tactics in off-table daily encounters, many readers may expect to study these pages for profit without having had any experience at poker.

It's surely conceivable that many readers are *mostly* interested in the non-poker benefits and are only reluctantly willing to wrestle with poker itself. If so, it would be very cruel to assume everyone's thorough knowledge from the outset.

That's why—quite cleverly, I think—I've decided to begin by telling you what poker is. Even if you already know poker in your heart, don't go away. Read this and you might gain a new perspective.

Poker...poker...how can I describe poker? Here, poker is...poker, you see...Let me think for a second...okay! I've decided not to begin with a definition. Instead, I'm going to describe a game of poker.

* * *

It's dark. I'm not talking about dark in some vacant field you might happen to be crossing by moonlight. I'm talking about real honest-to-goodness, can't-see-nothin' dark. You're on a lake in a rowboat. Alone! This is so scary, it's hard to keep writing . . . .

Why are you on the lake? Good question. You're crossing the lake because that's what you do every evening on your way back from Milwaukee, where you work as a remote adviser to the President. You're headed for a small settlement in Michigan where you live; and, like always, you're carrying lots of important government secrets. Obviously, the President trusts you very much. (Poker parlance: You have an ante invested in the pot.)

Since we're dealing with Lake Michigan, which is bigger than some might guess, typically it takes almost a half-hour to row across it. When the weather's bad or there's a lot of traffic, the same trip can take you a full hour and, believe me, your arms get tired.

Tonight there's hardly anyone else out there rowing, and the water is as calm as an empty bathtub. You'd be in high spirits if it weren't so damn dark. (Poker parlance: You can't see anyone else's hand.)

It occurs to me that some of my readers will have trouble picturing themselves rowing a boat across Lake Michigan in the dark, armed with government secrets.

It's my job as your teacher to make things easy to visualize. Try this. You're rowing the boat across Lake Michigan, armed with government secrets, as before, BUT it is not pitch black out there. Instead, you're wearing matching eye patches which prevent you from seeing the little starlight that exists. Maybe you'll be more comfortable with this latter imagery.

On with the story. You get about 50 miles from shore when you hear this whooshing. The whooshing sounds very much like your own oars carving through the peaceful waters. But, in fact, what you hear are not your own oars but almost an echo. . . nearer and nearer. Some other rowboat is approaching! (Poker parlance: Another player is out there putting his ante in the pot.)

You stop rowing and hold dead in the water. The alien oars splash closer and closer until you feel jarred as the other vessel bumps yours; then comes the sound of wood sliding on wood as, to your right, the intruding boat hugs your boat and lingers. (Poker parlance: The cards are now being dealt.)

"Get away!" you cry using your most authoritative voice. (Poker parlance: "Please don't bet.")

"Is your name. . ." astoundingly, a gruff male voice completes his query by using your name.

"How did you know that?" you demand.

"I may be blind, but I'm not stupid! I think you're carrying government documents, and I want them." (Poker parlance: "I may not know what you have, but you don't know what I have either, so I'll build myself a pot.")

Suddenly you know that the very secrets you're guarding for your President are in danger. A mighty tingle travels through your spine, then repeats the trek. (Poker parlance: You realize your opponent is about to bet, and you don't like it.)

These few seconds of silence are too much for the impatient man and he barks, "Well, are you carrying government documents or aren't you?" (Poker parlance: "Do you have a hand strong enough to gamble with me?")

"That's none of your business." (Poker parlance: "That's none of your business.")

"I'll make it my business, lady. I have a brick in my boat, and if you don't hand over the documents I'm going to stand as tall as I can and drop this brick into your boat. It will make a hole in the bottom, and you'll slowly sink and drown like a rat!" Here he heaves a manly cackle. (Poker parlance: "I bet $10.")

You sit silently and ponder your predicament. You cannot see, either because you're wearing eye patches or there's no trace of starlight (your choice, remember?) And the blind man cannot see, because. . .well, you know the reason.

"Hand over the documents!" the man insists.

After another pause, the man says, "I have *two* bricks in my boat, and if you don't give me those documents, I'm going to stand way up on my tiptoes and drop both into your boat. That will make two big holes, your boat will sink in seconds and you'll drown like a *scared* rat!" (Poker parlance: "I drew and helped my hand. Now I bet $50!")

A short surge of terror invades your being, but you fight it off. You think swiftly. Perhaps the man really does have two bricks. But what if he doesn't have any? You'd be giving up the secret documents just because a strange voice demanded them. (Poker parlance: Should you let this man win your $10 plus your ante just because he bet $50? He might be bluffing.)

"I'm keeping the President's papers!" you decide. "But I've got to warn you that I'm wearing pointy shoes. So, if you drop any bricks into my boat, I'm going to leap up while I'm sinking and kick you in the nuts." (Poker parlance: "I call your $50 and raise $10,000.")

It's a good thing he can't see that you're wearing only soft-toed tennis shoes. (Poker parlance: You're definitely bluffing.)

After some time for consideration, the alien voice seems meek: "How do I know you're *really* wearing pointy shoes?" (Poker parlance: "Do you really have a hand that good?")

Feeling that you're now in command, you reply, "You'll know when the time comes." (Poker parlance: "Call and find out!")

Now there comes the slow whoosing of oars through water. The sound grows more and more distant until you are again alone on Lake Michigan. (Poker parlance: "You win the pot.")

Now, either the moon slides from behind the clouds or you remove your eye patches (whichever applies). You focus on the home shore of Lake Michigan. And merrily you row your boat.

* * *

You'll be pleased to learn that, for the rest of this book, my analogies linking poker to the world beyond will be much more commonplace. The advanced winning tactics you'll learn will be available to you many times each day, whether or not you live near Lake Michigan. Think about the last few encounters you've had with men when the outcome really mattered. Chances are that many elements of a poker game were there, but you didn't realize it.

Had you been aware that poker was being played, you would have been able to use the tactics described on the following pages to destroy your male opponents.

Now let's take poker seriously.

Chapter Two

The Elements of Poker

At the back of this book, I've included a glossary of some poker terms I think you may need. Use it as often as you want; the service is free.

Here's what a standard 52-card deck looks like ....

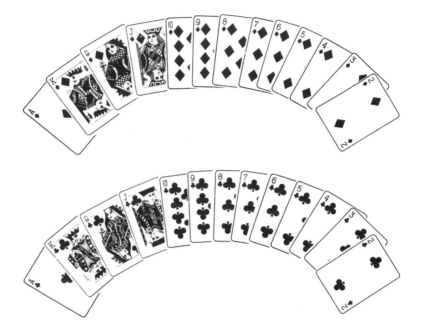

Every card has two attributes, called suit and rank. Each row of cards is of one suit. Although all suits have equal value (none is ranked higher than another), suits are important in poker because when the cards you hold are all the same suit, you have a powerful hand—called a flush (more on that later).

The suit symbols and their indentifiers are:

"Spades"   ♠

"Hearts"   ♥

"Diamonds"   ♦

"Clubs"   ♣

The first illustration was that of a full standard deck of 52 cards. Pick a row and scan it from left to right. The leftmost card, called an *ace*, is the highest ranking. Remember, the ace of spades, ace of hearts, ace of diamonds and ace of clubs all have the same value. They are tied for highest rank in the deck. As you scan to the right, each card is one rank lower than the card to its left.

The common names of the ranks, from left to right, are: ace, king, queen, jack, ten, nine, eight, seven, six, five, four, three or (sometimes) trey, two or (usually) deuce.

There are many popular variations of poker. Let's begin by looking at the one that's most widely known. It's called *five-card draw,* and practically everyone who plays any kind of poker knows how to play draw. Later in the book, we'll talk about other forms of poker and some strategy specific to them. However, in general, poker is poker, so let's learn "draw" first.

If you've never sat in a poker game before, here's what to expect. In draw poker, look for a table with from two to nine chairs around it. Typically, there will be eight chairs, but if you're playing "heads-up," which is poker for two, you only need one chair for each player, plus a third if you're using a neutral dealer.

In public poker rooms, eight players are standard. If the players take turns dealing the cards, there will be only eight seats. A ninth seat is often added when a neutral professional dealer is present.

Continuing to get all this good elementary stuff out of the way, let me tell you that there are three shapes of tables: round, oval and octagonal. If you're not quite sure what octagonal is, visualize a common, everyday eight-sided stop sign. Octagon-shaped poker tables are nice because, by nature of their design, they clearly define a territory for each player to sit and to organize his or her cards, chips and money.

Round tables require territorial estimates, but that's not a major problem. The same is true of oval tables, which are designed especially for employment of a professional dealer who sits in a special area in back of the table. Pro dealers at oval tables often have metal racks indented in the table in front of them. The racks allow them to keep chips for sale.

Now, suppose you walk up to a poker table to try your luck for the first time at five-card draw. Just to get things started, we'll assume yours is an octagonal table and no pro dealer is supplied. This means you'll have to deal the cards to the other players when your turn arrives.

Sit down. That wasn't so bad. See, everyone's smiling. There's one other woman at the table; she's 93-years-old and she gives you a kindly wink. A 35-year-old man in a blue business suit offers to buy you a cup of coffee. You say okay. (Good decision. This is going to cost him much more than the cup of coffee, but we'll cover that later.)

A waitress is summoned. The man says, "Bring me a tall glass of milk and the lady will have a cup of coffee."

"How 'bout me, Sonny? Ain't you gonna buy me no coffee?" the elderly lady quizzes more or less goodnaturedly.

The businessman laughs quite loudly. "Sure, Mrs. Edwards. Just tell the girl here how you want it."

The whole table seems cheerful. This is friendly poker, and while it's not exactly nickel limit, this lesson can't cost you much money. You take $10 out of your purse, the minimum buy-in, and buy a whole stack of chips from Mrs. Edwards.

She slides the chips across the table, you place them in front of you and suddenly some young cowboy shouts, "You can't do that! Put that money back on the table!"

The guy's rage is targeted at the elderly woman who was folding your $10 bill and heading for her pocketbook. A short argument ensues. It seems that the woman is violating poker law by taking money out of play. The rule here, as it is in most poker games, is that you can't remove any money from play until you quit and exchange your chips for money.

Things calm down quickly. Mrs. Edwards apologizes and places the $10 neatly beneath her many chips. You make a mental note: *Some poker players take the rules very seriously.*

10

A man three seats to your right is shuffling the cards. He does this by neatly putting all the cards in one stack, dividing the stack into two more or less equal halves and then riffling them in such a way as to make them intertwine somewhat randomly.

SUGGESTION: If you don't know how to shuffle or if you feel uncomfortable shuffling, practice! It won't take you long to develop this skill. In the meantime, it's probable that the kind people will allow you to pass your deal to the next player when it's your turn—or, maybe, you can talk another player into dealing for you. (Men like to do this for women.)

Anyway, in the situation you're imagining, you're very proud of your shuffle, because you've practiced it for half an hour last night. You know that it will be your turn to deal after just three hands are played, and you're ready.

The man three seats to your right has just finished shuffling and now he puts the entire stack of cards facedown in front of Mrs. Edwards. What he's doing is offering the cut. What's *cut?* It just so happens that, like every other important question posed on these pages, I know the answer.

Cut means to divide the deck into two parts.

After the dealer shuffles, he or she conventionally (and mandatorily, in most games) lets the player to the right cut. The dealer then exchanges the two parts of the deck by placing the part remaining in position after the cut on top of the section which the cutter has removed.

Thus, if the deck looks like this before the cut...

A
B
C
D
E

and the cutter takes the top two-thirds off and puts it to the side (traditionally *toward* the dealer), like this...

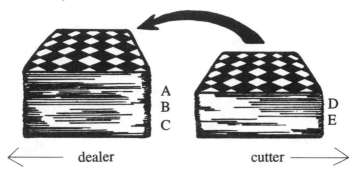

$\overset{\longleftarrow}{\text{dealer}}$ cutter $\longrightarrow$

Then the dealer changes the order of the deck by arranging it thus...

Cutting is intended to discourage cheating by preventing unscrupulous dealers from knowing the exact order of the cards through secret manipulation. That order is changed by the cut. Now the dealer begins by delivering one card off the top of the deck to Mrs. Edwards on his right.

"Wait! Hold it! Stop!" blurts the young cowboy. Everyone laughs. The dealer looks puzzled for a short moment, and then he realizes what he's done. He had begun begun to deal the cards to his right.

In poker, think *left*, which is *clockwise*. Almost everything happens in a clockwise manner—the next dealer is to the left of the current dealer, the cards are dealt one-by-one to the left and the betting begins at the left and continues to the right.

Now that the dealer has finished chastising himself he begins to distribute cards in the proper direction. We're almost ready to play our very first hand of poker.

Chapter Three

Your First Hand

The dealer distributes one card face down to everyone in turn. Face down means you can't see the ranks and suits. All you can see is a pretty design on the backs of the cards. These back-of-card designs are identical, so you can't tell one of the 52 cards from any other without looking at the reverse sides. In order for the players to know what the cards are, they'll have to pick them up and peek at them.

Completely circling the table, the dealer gives one card to each player, the last going to himself. But he doesn't stop after dealing everyone a card. Hell, no! This is poker and things are just getting started.

Without even a pause for breath, he continues past himself and delivers a second card to the player to his left, then a card to the player *two* seats to his left, and now *you* get a second card. What fun! And you haven't even looked at your first one yet!

"Stop!" cries the young cowboy. This time his manly finger is aimed in your direction. *Me? What did I do?* you wonder. "She didn't ante! She's tryin' to get away without anteing!"

"Ah, come on!" scolds the kind businessman to your right. "She didn't mean anything by it. She just forgot. We all forget sometimes."

Now you see what the problem is. Everyone has taken a red chip, valued at 25 cents, and put it forward onto the table. These antes should be entered by every player before the deal begins. They are the beginnings of what is called a *pot*—a collection of chips and money that players wager during the course of a poker hand. (Note that the term *hand* has two meanings in poker. It means your private collection of five cards—"your hand." And it means one individual game of poker—"the winner of the hand.") Eventually, the whole pot will go to just one winner of the hand (unless there's a tie, in which case the pot will be fairly divided). Antes are a token amount (in this case 25 cents per player for a total of $2) that seeds the pot and makes it worth fighting over. Without antes, there would be nothing to win and little incentive for anyone to make a first bet.

Anyway, having forgotten to ante, you quickly pick up one of the 10 white chips, worth $1 each that Mrs. Edwards sold you. You ask Sonny, the businessman next to you for change. He graciously gives you four red chips, and you slide one of these into the pot in front of you. You notice that all the chips are the same size, about that of a silver dollar (the large kind, not the Susan B. Anthony ones). They are lighter but sturdy, better constructed than some of the plastic poker chips you've seen in stores—though those are fine for informal home use.

"Let's keep the pot straight from now on," the cowboy insists. He wants to go to war with you. You smile sweetly, and surprised, he forces himself to return that smile. "Can I buy you a cup of coffee, lady?" he asks.

Sort of curtly, you say, "Sonny already bought me a cup," take a sip and gratefully tap Sonny on the arm. The cowboy says nothing and now you refuse to look at him. You haven't decided what kind of strategy to use against him, but at least you're playing games with his mind. He'll be confused and vulnerable later on.

Well, the dealer continues his interrupted circuit of the table and then keeps right on going. Everyone gets a third card. By now some players, including Mrs. Edwards and Sonny to your right, are peeking at their cards. They're doing this in a manner that makes it almost impossible for anyone except themselves to see the suits and ranks. You make a mental note: *Poker players like to keep their hands secret.*

What is a player's *hand*, exactly? Well, just hold on a second and you'll see. The dealer doesn't stop until each player has five cards. Those five cards comprise a standard poker hand. Everyone's looking at theirs now and your five cards are still on the table in front of you. Pick them them up, for godsake!

There, that's better. Careful! Shelter them with your hands while you're looking. You don't want anyone else to see them. Hold them like a fan. Notice that the cards are thin (all 52 cards stacked together measure roughly three-quarters of an inch from bottom to top), and very slick. Most cards that you buy at the drugstore are a sturdy paper that's been plastic coated. However, the cards you're now using are pure plastic. They're much more expensive (about $8 a deck compared to $1 for plastic coated), but they last a long time. They are, like most standard cards, about 3½ inches tall and 2½ inches wide and you find them easy to handle. Here's what your cards are . . .

After staring at these for several seconds, you feel you'd like to rearrange them so that they look like . . .

You begin to sort your poker hand. Don't! Experienced players seldom sort their poker hands. You could be giving information about your hand to alert opponents. I won't explain this right now. But after you understand the elements of poker, you'll be able to reason out for yourself why this is so. In the meantime, trust me—never rearrange your hand. Okay, you're looking at your hand, now what? Well, the first thing you must know is whether you hold a good, bad or medium hand.

We'd better take time out here and examine that.

Chapter Four

How to Rate Your Poker Hand

Conventions have been established which make certain combinations of five cards more valuable than other combinations.
One thing that doesn't matter at all is the order that the cards
appear in your hand.

For that reason...

all have the same value, because they are cards of identical ranks. Since the deck contains only one card of each exact rank coupled with an exact suit, you don't need to worry about two players getting identical hands. However, two or more players might get *similar* hands that have identical *values*. In the previous illustration, the three hands are identical, right down to the ranks and suits of the cards. Therefore, these could never turn up simultaneously in the same deal. What I want to emphasize by the illustration is that it doesn't change the value of your cards if you rearrange them. But sorting cards is a very bad poker habit.

Here are two similar poker hands that, at first glance look almost identical. In fact, they have identical values, as you'll soon learn.

If we want to understand the rankings of individual poker hands, we should first look at the most powerful hand in standard poker. This is it...

Wow! That's called a *royal flush* and it beats every hand that isn't a royal flush. After you get 100 years of poker experience behind you, I want you to try to imagine a better hand. You can't. Nobody can. There isn't any. If you ever get this hand, bet your life on it, because you cannot lose. Alas, it's not easy to get. In fact, for every four royal flushes you'll be dealt in your lifetime, you'll receive—on average—2,598,956 hands that are *not* royal flushes. If you don't intend to play much poker, there's a good chance you'll never pick up a royal flush, so admire the one I'm showing you.

What does it take for a poker hand to qualify as a royal flush? First, it must contain an ace (the highest ranking card), a king, a queen, a jack and a ten. That's easy to remember, because each card I mentioned after the ace is exactly one rank lower than the card before. Second, a royal flush must contain five cards of the same suit. The suit in the illustration was spades, but all hearts, all diamonds or all clubs would also have been a royal flush.

So let's start a list of the ranking of poker hands, by major categories, from best to worst.

So far our list looks thus...

1. Royal flush

So, what's the second best category of hand you can get in

poker? It turns out that the second best kind of hand is so similar to the first category that we could include both in the same definition. In fact, you could easily argue that there should be no separate category for royal flush. A royal flush is only the highest ranking member of a category called *straight flush*.

Here's how to identify a straight flush. First, when considered from highest rank to lowest rank, each following card must be exactly one rank lower than the previous card. For instance, nine-eight-seven-six-five or jack-ten-nine-eight-seven qualifies. Eight-seven-five-four-three does *not* qualify because there's a difference of two ranks (rather than one) between the seven and the five. Second, for the hand to rate proudly as a straight flush all of its five cards must be of the same suit.

These are straight flushes...

Remember, it doesn't matter if the cards are arranged in an orderly sequence, highest to lowest. They are judged on whether they *could be* so arranged.

Whenever your cards can be organized from highest to lowest

in ranks of exactly one less than the card before, you have a *straight* (more later). Any time all five of your cards are of the same suit, you have a *flush* (more later). When you have both of these things at the same time, you have a straight flush, which is so powerful that it makes me tremble to talk about it.

Now you see why, by definition, a royal flush is just another version of a straight flush. It is a straight flush that has an ace as its highest-ranking card.

This is not a straight flush...

because there are not five cards of the same suit. If the five of clubs were a five of diamonds, then you'd have a straight flush. What you see here is a plain, ordinary straight, but that's still a pretty powerful hand.

What happens if there are two or more straight flushes in the same hand? Which hand is better? Well, you won't see that happen much, but the player with the highest ranking card wins.

For instance...

Beats...

The first is called a queen-high straight flush; the second, a ten-high straight flush. Since queen ranks higher than ten, the first hand wins. This high-card method is also used to determine winners when there's a tie for best category with a straight or flush (or even *no pair*, a category you shouldn't think about yet). The method won't resolve all high-hand disputes.

These two hands are tied in importance...

Remember, all suits have equal value, so spades can't beat hearts or vice versa.

This might be a good time to jar you with a strange reality. The following hand is also a straight flush . . .

If you're new to poker, I understand the torment you must be going through at this moment. No matter how you mentally arrange those cards, you can't find anything that fits the definition of a straight flush.

Ah, but there is a straight flush there, and this is what it looks like unscrambled . . .

You see, there is a special exception to the governing laws of poker which allows the ace (normally the highest ranking card) to be considered lower than the deuce (also known as a two—the lowest ranking card) *if* the ace can be used on the low end of a five-high straight flush or a plain ordinary five-high straight. (Ordinary straights will be discussed soon. They're simply straight flushes without the matching suits.)

This mysterious versatility of the ace might cause you to believe that the rankings "wrap around" and allow you to have straight flushes such as . . .

The reasoning is that the three is higher than the deuce (two), the deuce can be construed as being higher than an ace for straight flushes and straights and, at that point, an ace is higher than a king (as it usually is) and a king higher than a queen. The sequence is preserved, so is it a straight flush?

No! Unfortunately for those who like to make straight flushes, the wrap-around effect using an ace both high and low is not legal. There is only *one* special circumstance when an ace is low. *Only one.* When you're creating a straight flush or a straight, the exact ranks of five-four-three-deuce-ace *must* exist for the ace to be low. In all other situations, the ace is high.

Our rankings so far. . .

1. Royal flush

2. Straight flush

What's next? This is next. . .

That's called *four of a kind* and any time you get it you can figure you're probably going to earn some money. In order to have four of a kind, four of your five cards must be identical in rank. If two (or more) players are tied in category for best hand with four of a kind, then the higher ranking four of a kind wins. The rank of the fifth card is not relevant, because no two players can hold four of a kind of identical ranks. (There are only four of each rank in the deck.)

This four of a kind...

Beats this four of a kind...

even though the second, losing, hand has the single highest ranking card, a king. That king has no importance. It is the relative ranks of four of a kind that determine the winner. In the example, queens win by outranking jacks.

Our list...

1. Royal flush

2. Straight flush

3. Four of a kind

A *full house* is awesome as a hand. It ranks fourth among poker categories and here is what one looks like...

Even though we shouldn't rearrange our hands in the course of a poker game, let me sort this illustration for you to make our discussion easier.

There, that's better. As you can clearly see, this full house is made up of three cards of one rank and two cards of another. In fact, all full houses can be so defined. This hand is called tens-full, because ten is the rank of the *three* matching cards. It is that consideration which is important if you have two or more full houses tied for best category. The one with the high-ranking three matching cards wins.

You don't have to worry about the remaining twin-ranking cards, because the rank of the *three* matching cards is the determining factor. It's impossible to have two full houses with the same rank of three matching cards. For instance, to have two tens-full (full houses with three tens included) competing for the same pot, there would need to be six tens in the deck. There aren't; there are only four.

Note that this is not a full house...

because, even though there are three of one rank (queens), there are not twins of another rank to go with them.

With these two full houses...

the second one (tens-full) would win, despite the fact that the highest cards (aces) belong to the nines-full. The three tens are higher than the three nines, and that's all that matters. The two aces don't count, except for qualifying the first hand as a full

house—which *any* two cards of the same rank would do as well.
Our list. . .

1. Royal flush

2. Straight flush

3. Four of a kind

4. Full house

Next comes a *flush*. The only requirements for a flush are that
all five cards be of the same suit and the hand not be *better* than
a flush (i.e. a straight flush or a royal flush).

This is a flush. . .

This is not a flush. . .

because it is much better than a flush. It is a straight flush.

And this is not a flush...

because only four of the five cards are of the same suit. A flush requires *all five* cards to be of matching suits. Four out of five won't even earn sympathy.

If two or more flushes tie for best category, the winner would be the one with the highest card. In this case...

the first hand is better because it contains an ace, whereas the second hand's high-ranking card is only a king.

If two or more flushes have identical-ranking high cards, the second-highest card in each hand is used to determine the winner. And if that second card still leaves the hands tied, the third-highest card makes the difference, and so forth. So...

beats...

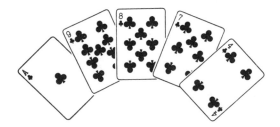

because the tie is broken by comparison of second-highest-ranking cards, a ten beating a nine.

In the following two hands...

we cannot determine the better hand until we get to the fifth and last card and see that a four outranks a three.

On very rare occasions, two (or possibly more) flushes may tie for best hand and the pot must be equally divided between the winners. These hands tie...

Our list so far...

1. Royal flush
2. Straight flush
3. Four of a kind
4. Full house
5. Flush

Another really happy hand is a *straight*. If you pick one up, you should usually be willing to do a little gambling with it. It's the kind of hand you should expect to lose with sometimes, but overall it will win more often than it will lose and it brings you a long range profit.

Here's a straight . . .

Remember, it probably won't arrive in that exact order, so you'll have to sort it out in your mind. After a little practice you'll learn to do this quickly and you won't even consider physically rearranging your cards.

To qualify as a straight, the cards must be capable of being arranged in descending order starting with the highest rank and continuing through the lowest with every card, after the first one, ranking exactly one lower than the card before it.

If all five cards are also the same suit, you have a straight flush and not a straight, and perhaps you should be proud. Remember the special condition we talked about earlier: If you hold this hand . . .

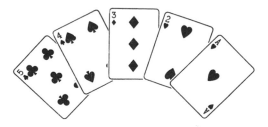

you have a straight. That's because the ace can be construed as low if you have exactly a five, a four, a three and a deuce to go with it. (See the discussion of straight flushes.) If there are two or more straights vying for a pot, the highest-ranking one wins. Just to make this clear as a clean sky, there are only ten different flavors of straights, and here's an example of each one, rated from best to worst (and even the worst is usually good enough to win money)...

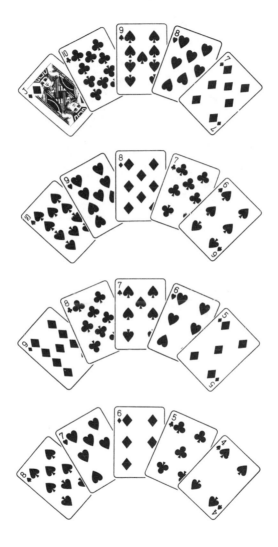

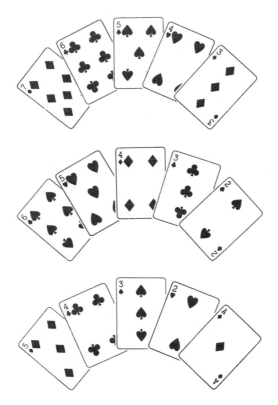

Those are the only kinds of straights you'll ever see, even if you have a great deal of patience. Remember, a straight can never have two cards of the same rank in it. Sometimes beginners think a hand like eight-seven-seven-six-five is a straight, but it isn't. Each card after the first must be *one lower* in rank—not the same rank *or* one lower.

Now our list of categories looks like this . . .

1. Royal flush

2. Straight flush

3. Four of a kind

4. Full house

5. Flush

6. Straight

Next comes *three of a kind*, which is like a full house without the two extra matching cards. Here are some hands that rate as three of a kind...

In the order of their appearance, they are three sevens, three aces and three queens. If two or more players have three of a kind, the best hand is determined by the rank of each three of a kind and nothing more. Three sevens are better than three sixes, no matter what the remaining cards are in each hand.

This three of a kind...

wins over this three of a kind...

even though the second hand somehow looks stronger with the ace and king present. Those extra cards don't matter. Nines beat eights, period.

Our list...

1. Royal flush

2. Straight flush

3. Four of a kind

4. Full house

5. Flush

6. Straight

7. Three of a kind

Now we arrive at a category called *two pair.* You may feel in your heart that we're scraping the bottom of the barrel because there are so many higher categories than two pair and, as you'll see, not many below it. However, when you pick up the five cards the dealer has given you and you look at them, there's only one chance in 13 that you'll have a hand as good as two pair. That's because, although there's a lot of categories above two pair, they're hard to get.

There's nothing terrible about two pair if you know what you're doing.

Here are some examples of two pair...

When there are two or more players tied with two pair, how do we know who's best? First, you must know that the term *pair* means exactly two cards of the same rank. A six and a six is a pair. A jack and a jack is a pair. A heart and a heart is *not* a pair, because only ranks, not suits, are considered in determining pairs. When you have two pair, you have two individual pairs. To determine the better hand when you and an opponent both have two pairs, you examine which one of you holds the highest of the four pairs (i.e. your two pairs plus your opponent's two pairs).

If your opponent's hand is . . .

and your hand is . . .

then your hand is better because kings (your high pair) ranks above queens (your opponent's high pair). In such a case neither your lower pair or your unpaired cards makes any difference. However, sometimes the top pair can be the same in both hands.

Here, I'll show you . . .

In this case, the first hand wins. Both players have the same high pair, so the better hand is determined by examining the low pairs. Sixes beat fives, so the issue is decided. Rarely, two players can have hands in which both their high pairs and their low pairs are the same. Then, the extra card determines the winner.

This hand . . .

is not quite as good as this hand...

Once in a great while players will have hands consisting of exactly the same two pair with the extra card also of identical ranks. In such a case, the hands are tied.

We're getting close to the end of our list now...

1. Royal flush

2. Straight flush

3. Four of a kind

4. Full house

5. Flush

6. Straight

7. Three of a kind

8. Two pair

One pair is next, and it's exactly what you think it is. These hands rank as one pair...

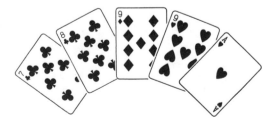

In order of appearance, these hands are called a pair of nines, a pair of aces and a pair of tens. If more than one hand has one pair, the winner (assuming no other active player has a hand of a higher category) is determined by the high pair. A pair of nines is absolutely better than a pair of sevens, no matter what the other cards in the two hands are. A pair of queens is absolutely better than a pair of jacks. A pair of aces is better than any other kind of pair.

If two players have the same pair, the better one-pair hand is determined by looking at the extraneous cards.

This hand . . .

beats this hand...

because a jack beats a ten. When the pairs tie, the high extraneous card is used to find the winner and the other two lower extraneous cards in each hand don't matter. If the highest of the three non-paired cards is the same in both identically paired hands, then the next high-ranking card determines the winner. And if those are the same, then the last card is used to break the tie. Rarely, a tie cannot be broken and the pot is divided.

Using these rules, this hand...

beats this hand...

because the three of diamonds beats the deuce of spades.
  These two hands tie...

We're almost done with our list...

1. Royal flush
2. Straight flush
3. Four of a kind
4. Full house
5. Flush
6. Straight
7. Three of a kind
8. Two pair
9. One pair

Now we must examine the saddest hand of all in poker. It's called *no pair*. It's the lowest category, reserved only for hands that have no other home. A straight or a flush (or a straight flush or a royal flush, for that matter) is not known as no pair, even though there can never be a pair within a straight or a flush. (Why can't you have a pair and a flush at the same time? Because both cards of the pair would have to be of the same suit, and that's impossible with the 52-card deck as we've defined it.)

If a hand qualifies in none of the nine categories already defined, it falls into the 10th and final no-pair category.

Here are some no pair hands...

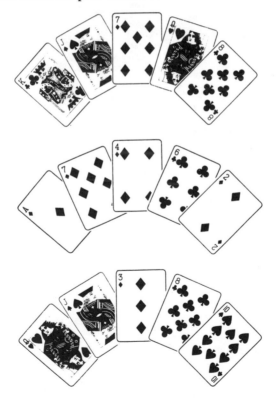

Occasionally, circumstances may dictate that two hands of no pair are the final contenders for the pot. The winner is then decided by high cards. The highest card from one hand is matched against the highest card from the other. If a better-ranking card is found, the winner is instantly decided. If the high cards are the same, the second-highest cards in each hand are matched and if necessary, the third-highest cards are tested, or even the fourth- or fifth-highest.

Using this method, this hand...

loses to this hand....

And this hand...

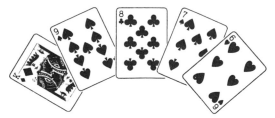

beats this hand...

although the winner cannot be determined until the final cards are examined. These two no pair hands tie...

Here, then, is the final list of poker categories, rated according to strength...

1. Royal flush

2. Straight flush

3. Four of a kind

4. Full house

5. Flush

6. Straight

7. Three of a kind

8. Two pair

9. One pair

10. No pair

Now let's get back to your hand in progress and see if we can win it.

Chapter Five

Back to the Table

"You're holding up the game, lady." The young cowboy sounds exasperated. Remember that he had been hostile at first, then you smiled at him, then you refused to continue with that unexpected kindness. I mean, this cow puncher is really confused. He tips his hat backward and brushes back a few stray strands of hair.

"It's up to you," says Mrs. Edwards, nodding your way. Sure, you've taken too much time to act on your hand, but what do they expect? You just read a lengthy explanation of the relative rankings of poker hands. Did they think you could do that in three seconds?

Some important things have happened since we last scanned the poker table. The player to the left of the dealer (two seats to your right), an elderly man who perpetually trembles, has made a fist and rapped it somewhat firmly against the top of the table.

This did not startle anyone. It seemed to be the sort gesture they expected. You must understand that gesture in order to play poker effectively. What the elderly man did is called *checking*.

After the dealer had finished distributing five cards to each player, himself included, it was time for the poker hand to be played. Since poker is an orderly game, everyone does not act at once. Players take turns. In poker, the player to the dealer's left gets first chance to act on his hand. Remember, most things in poker happen in a clockwise manner.

The player immediately to the dealer's left is the elderly man and he had these options as the first player to act:

1. He could make an opening bet; or

2. He could check.

He chose to check. Had he done so by declaring, "option number two," nobody would understand what he meant except, maybe, a few who'd read this book. Obviously, some other means must be available to declare that you're checking, and, by golly, such other means do exist! One way to check is by rapping the table. You can make a fist, but that isn't required. Almost any gesture with your hand against the table would get the message across to your opponents. The elderly man elected to make a fist and rap his knuckles firmly against the top of the table. He didn't hurt himself, because typical poker tables, including this one, are heavily padded and covered with felt or canvas.

He could have also said the word "check." He could have said, "pass," which in this case would mean the same thing. He might have muttered, "you go ahead," meaning that the next player should act—in effect, he would be checking. He might simply have pointed or otherwise gestured to the next player.

You see, there are many ways any player might let you know that he or she is checking. Those ways are all valid in poker as long as they're understood. If the words or gestures (or combinations of words and gestures) are not understood, then players will usually ask for a clarification.

Now you should be able to recognize when a player is checking, but what does *check* mean? Check means that you are declining to bet at this time, but reserve the right to call or raise (these terms discussed later) someone else's bet, should there be one. You can only check if nobody else has made a bet already. Looking ahead a little, if you are faced with an opposing bet, you must:

1. Call it;

2. Raise it; or

3. Pass.

The elderly man was not faced with an opposing bet, so he had only the option of making an initial bet himself or checking. He decided to check, thus waiting to see what the other players would do when their turns arrived.

If nobody has bet when it's your turn to act, you may:

1. Make a bet; or

2. Check.

If somebody has already bet when it's your turn to act, you may:

1. Call (putting into the pot an amount equal to the bet);

2. Raise (putting into the pot an amount equal to the bet plus some more); or

3. Pass (throwing your cards away and relinquishing any chance whatsoever of winning the pot).

If you're unfamiliar with poker, these concepts will become clearer as we continue our first hand. Bringing you up to date— after the elderly man checked, the right to act passed clockwise. It was then up to Sonny—your new friend, the businessman—to decide what to do. After several seconds he decided to bet.

The game you're sitting in is limit poker, which means there is a rule governing how much a bet can be. In this case, the rule is that you can bet no more or less than one white chip—$1. In other words, the amount of Sonny's bet must be $1; he has no option as to how big a wager he can make. That is a very common kind of poker. Limit poker is much more common than no-limit. Sometimes, the rules of limit poker say that you can bet any amount in a range of, say, $1 to $10. If that were the case, then there would be more planning and strategy required in selecting the amount to bet. Here, Sonny must either bet $1 or bet nothing at all, and he has chosen to bet.

He places his white chip out in front of him so it's clear that it's a wager and belongs with the rest of the pot. He says, "open." *Open?* What's that? Don't ask me, ask Sonny. And you'd better find out fast, because with all this talking I've done between when the dealer passed out the first card and now, we really are taking too long. I apologize. We're being rude to the table.

You turn to Sonny. "What did you mean when you said, 'open'?" Unexpectedly, Sonny turns out to be not just an ordinary businessman, but a professional orator, one of fewer than 50 you've ever met. He stands up and begins to speak. Everyone seems awed by the elegance of his posture and the finesse of his tiniest gestures. Here stands a man you can believe in.

"To begin with," and here you note that his voice is so very polished, "I must beg you to understand that for every game of poker that's played, there can be only one winner—barring a tie of course—and one pot and...," he points at himself, "...one opener. And right now it's me. To open simply means you make the first bet. When a pot is stripped bare of everything except its primordial...," he really drags out the word, indicating that he is quite fond of it, "...antes, then anyone can open. But only once! Only once!" He points to you, wanting you to repeat his last words.

"Only once," you say.

"So how many openers are there in a pot?" he demands.

"Only one," you answer.

"And how many times can that one opener open?"

"Only once."

"And who is the opener in this pot?"

"You are."

"Now it's your turn," he says and abruptly takes his seat.

There is warm applause from the other players, except the young cowboy who groans, "Quit wastin' time."

"There's something else she should know," offers Mrs. Edwards.

"Sonny couldn't have opened without openers."

Openers? What are openers? Since I'm sitting with my fingers on the keyboard, I could really do you a disservice here. I could have Mrs. Edwards stand up and tell you about openers, but she's not a professional orator, like Sonny, so let me explain.

The rules of poker differ from game to game. In some five-card draw games (that's the form of poker you're presently playing), you can open with any kind of hand imaginable.

If you were feeling reckless, it would be legal for you to open with this hand...

which doesn't have a pair or even an ace in it.

Remember, the category called *no pair* is the very lowest ranking of all standard poker categories. What you've just seen is a really bad poker hand. Still, in some games it's perfectly permissible to open with that hand if you're determined to do it.

More likely, your five-card draw game will be governed by a rule which forbids opening with less than some minimum strength of hand. By far the most common implementation of this rule is called *jacks or better to open* or *jacks or better* for short.

When this rule is active, as it is in your present game, no one can open without a hand at least this strong...

You could not open with either of these hands . . .

To open legally requires a hand that fits, at least, into the category of one pair with a pair that is, at least, as high as jacks.

Sonny has opened, so you already know something about his hand. You know that he can beat a pair of tens. You also know that the strength of his hand is somewhere in the range of a pair of jacks up to a royal flush.

It is important to understand a little about the probabilities of poker here. *It is much more likely that the actual hand Sonny holds is near the low end of that range than near the high end.*

> IN THE REAL WORLD BEYOND POKER, YOU
> SHOULD USUALLY ASSUME THAT THE BARGAIN-
> ING POSITION OF ANY ADVERSARY IS NEARER
> THE LOW END THAN THE HIGH END OF A POSSI-
> BLE RANGE. THIS IS ESPECIALLY TRUE OF MEN
> WHOSE EGOS ARE THREATENED BY YOU. WE'LL
> DISCUSS THESE CONCEPTS LATER.

You must keep in mind that Sonny, or any average player who opened is more likely to have two pair or one pair than anything stronger. Now let's decide what to do with your hand. Well, we haven't looked at it for quite some time, so let's take another peek and refresh our memories.

Here are your cards, after we mentally arranged them in an easy-to-view order. . .

You probably recognize that your hand falls into one of the ten categories of poker strength. Specifically, it is two pair. Not just any two pair, either. You have a very high ranking two-pair hand—aces and sevens. Conventionally, poker players call this hand "aces up." They seldom bother to identify the second pair unless it becomes necessary to break a tie. Kings up means two pair with the high pair being kings; sixes up means a pair of sixes and some smaller pair.

How strong is aces up? Pretty strong. For every 28 hands you're dealt, you'll only get a hand as good as aces up once, on average. That will take about 40 minutes at the fairly brisk rate at which public poker is played (i.e.,40 to 48 competitive hands dealt per hour).

It's your turn to act, so let's examine your options:

1. You can call by putting in the same amount that Sonny bet—$1.

2. You can raise Sonny by putting in $2.

3. You can pass.

If you choose to call, it will cost you $1 and you'll remain in contention for the pot. Then all five players who have not had a chance to act on their hands will decide, in turn, whether to call, raise or pass. Finally, the elderly man who first checked will get a second chance to act. He can then call, raise or pass; but he cannot check again since he's faced with a bet. (Remember, you can only check and see what happens if no one else has bet already.)

If you choose to raise, you must wager $2. The first dollar equals the bet made by Sonny. The second $1 is the raise. In the form of limit poker you're engaged in, all bets and raises (on this betting round) must be by increments of one dollar. If you raise, all players would need to at least call your raise to stay in contention. Any player, except Sonny, who entered the pot would be required to wager $2. Sonny would only need to call your $1 raise, because he's already wagered $1. There are many reasons why you might want to raise a pot. In general, though, and these are the three main ones:

1.   You raise to win more money from players who've already bet. If you hold a really strong poker hand and someone bets $1, you might feel that you'd rather try to win $2 from that person, and so you raise hoping he'll put another dollar into the pot you expect to win.

2.   You raise to keep too many players from entering the pot. Cer-

tain poker hands make better profit in the long run when played against only two players (more later). You may then raise to make it too expensive for new players, who haven't invested anything yet, to enter the pot.

3. You raise as a *bluff*. When you're bluffing, you have no reasonable expectation of holding the best hand. You hope to win by default if no player has the will or the courage to call your raise. (Bluffing is also frequently done not by raising, but simply by betting hoping no one will call.)

You see, in poker, ALL PLAYERS COMPETING FOR A POT MUST INVEST AN EQUAL AMOUNT OR THE PLAYER WHO HAS BET THE MOST MONEY WINS BY DEFAULT. (There are special rules to handle situations where players don't have the amount of the bet available. Let's talk about that later.) If there's a bet, you must always call, raise or surrender (i.e. pass).

Presently, you can choose neither to call nor to raise, but, rather, to pass. If you do, you must throw your cards face down onto the center of the table, thus eliminating yourself from any chance of winning. Not having any chance of winning a pot is obviously a horrible disadvantage, but there's one great benefit—you can't lose any more money.

So here you are with aces up. What to do? You definitely shouldn't pass, since you probably have a better hand than Sonny, who opened. That means you must either raise or call. It turns out that either choice is acceptable in this situation. Since we're not presently evaluating poker on an advanced strategic level, I'll leave it up to you.

Fine, you decided to call. No sense getting too aggressive until you're more familiar with your surroundings.

Immediately after you call, everyone else passes through and including the dealer. By passing they forfeit any rights to the pot. That means that the contest has narrowed to just you and Sonny. Well, almost. Of course, there's the elderly man with palsy, but you figure there's not much chance he'll play, because he already had one opportunity to bet and chose, instead, to check. You sort of hope he doesn't call, because you have a strong hand with aces up and you'd feel bad about taking money from this frequently smiling elderly gentleman.

"I raise!" growls that same elderly gentlemen. His voice sounds none too kindly now. What's going on here, you wonder. Hey, it's just that way with poker. It's a funny game, and it makes people do funny things. Don't worry about it. The old man slides in his two bucks and waits for Sonny, whose turn it is, to decide what to do.

Can the old man do that? you wonder, studying him incredulously. Sure, he can. In poker, if you check and someone else bets, you have every right to raise. That's part of the thrill and the tension of the game. You never know what you're stepping into when you prance into a pot. One word of caution: Make sure you understand any special rules which apply to your present game. Sometimes it is not legal to check and later raise. But the more common practice is that checking and then raising if someone else bets is perfectly acceptable. In your game, it certainly seems to be legal, because the old man has just done it. By the way, the practice of checking and then raising is often called *sandbagging*. It is not popular among some naive poker players, but professionals universally endorse it as a strategic option which adds intrigue to the game.

CHECKING AND THEN RAISING IS ONE OF THE MOST POWERFUL TACTICS INTELLIGENT PEOPLE CAN USE IN THE REAL WORLD BEYOND POKER. WHEN WOMEN USE IT SELECTIVELY AGAINST MEN, THE ADVANTAGES ARE EVEN GREATER.

After several seconds of hesitation, Sonny decides to pass. He tosses his cards face down onto the center of the table. He is out of the pot. Totally out! He has no more claim to the money and his original $1 bet (plus his quarter ante) has been forever forfeited.

Now it's up to you. Your aces up are almost certainly better than whatever hand Sonny folded, but is it good enough to beat the old man?

Probably not. Then you should pass, right? Probably not. But why risk another $1 if you probably have the losing hand? Odds, that's why. There's $4 in bets out there ($2 from the old man and $1 each from you and Sonny) plus $2 in total 25-cent antes. That means the pot is $6 large and either you're going to win it or the old man's going to win it. True, you're probably going to lose, but that isn't what you should consider here. Evaluating this pot on the basis of whether you're probably going to win or lose is one of the costliest mistakes you can make in poker.

EVALUATING A REAL WORLD SITUATION SOLELY ON THE BASIS OF WHETHER YOU'RE GOING TO WIN OR LOSE IS, LIKEWISE, VERY COSTLY. IN LIFE AND IN POKER YOU MUST ANALYZE IMPORTANT DECISIONS ON THE BASIS OF HOW FREQUENTLY YOU EXPECT TO WIN RELATIVE TO WHAT SUCCESS WILL PAY YOU. YOU MIGHT THINK YOU ONLY HAVE ONE CHANCE IN 20 OF SUCCEEDING, BUT YOU STILL DECIDE TO CONTINUE THE EFFORT BECAUSE THE REWARDS ARE MUCH GREATER THAN 20 TO 1. ALWAYS KEEP THIS CONCEPT IN MIND. ALWAYS.

Go ahead and call the old man. I'm not saying that you should always call in a similar situation with aces up, but I know this old guy and he raises frequently enough on small two pair that this is worth the call. Trust me. Well, I see that you're hesitating. You don't want to invest that extra dollar. Look at it this way. Let's say you run into a similar poker situation five times. You put in the extra dollar each time. Sadly, you only win once and lose four times. Well, that's not so sad, when you think about it! The one time you win, you take the whole pot, which amounts to the $6 that was there when you decided to call the old man's raise, plus the returned $1 that you called with. You earned $6 that you could never have won had you passed. Conversely, four times you lost the extra $1 used to call the raise. So for the five hands, you lost $1 four times (minus $4) and you won $6 once (plus $6). You're $2 ahead by making the extra $1 call. Even though you're still not ahead overall for those five hands (considering that it cost you $2 in total bets plus a 25-cent ante each time), you *are* ahead on the specific decision to call the extra $1. And that's the only decision you're faced with now.

Come on, call. You'll still have $7.75 left of the $10 you started with. Even if you lose, you'll have $7.75. Go ahead, it's only a dollar! There, that wasn't so bad. Hold it! Don't turn your cards face up yet. More good stuff is about to happen. We're going to *draw cards!*

Chapter Six

Drawing to Your Hand

This is the really exciting part of five-card draw poker. If you don't like the hand you have, you can draw to make a better one—thus the derivation of the name, *draw*. Here's what draw means: You can discard as many of your five cards as you see fit and get replacements. That means, if you didn't like any of the cards you were originally dealt, you could request five new ones. If you wanted to keep two cards, just throw away the rest and get three fresh cards. No matter how many new cards you desire, just tell the dealer and he'll fulfill your wish.

Maybe you think it's a big advantage for you to get this extra shot at improving your hand, but it isn't, because every *active* player (i.e., every player who hasn't passed and remains in contention for the pot) has an opportunity to draw. You thought you were the only one, huh? Maybe I misled you.

Right now, the elderly man (who is first to declare his draw because he is closer clockwise to the dealer), is deciding what to do. He raps a trembling fist against the top of the table.

Wait! Doesn't that mean check? Can the old man abstain from drawing until after you decide what to do? No, that's not what rapping the table means at this time. It's really unfortunate, but that gesture means two distinctly different things in poker:

1. Rapping the table when it's up to a player to *bet* means that player has decided to wait and see what the opponents do.

2. Rapping the table when it's time to *draw* cards means the player doesn't want any.

Definition two refers to a poker tactic commonly known as *standing pat,* among many similar labels (i.e., rapping pat, staying pat, playing a pat hand, etc.). You can draw five, four, three, two, one or you can stand pat. Those are your six options when it comes time to draw cards. In some games, the rules are that players can only draw four or sometimes three cards. But at your table today, you can draw all five if you want to.

ALWAYS MAKE SURE YOU KNOW WHAT THE SPECIAL RULES ARE WHEN YOU FIRST SIT DOWN TO PLAY IN AN UNFAMILIAR GAME. THE REAL WORLD VERSION OF THIS CONCEPT IS CRITICAL. MANY PEOPLE HABITUALLY LEARN ABOUT THE RULES GOVERNING THEIR DAILY CONFRONTATIONS AS THEY GO ALONG. THAT'S INCORRECT AND STRATEGICALLY COSTLY. TO WHATEVER EXTENT IT'S POSSIBLE, YOU SHOULD LEARN THE "RULES" BEFORE YOU PARTICIPATE IN ANY IMPORTANT ENCOUNTER. OFTEN, THERE WILL BE NO ESTABLISHED RULES AND YOU CAN SPECIFY YOUR OWN!

The old man has elected to stand pat, so let's examine what this might imply. He's saying he doesn't want any cards. Why not? Well, if he had a hand that was in the weakest category, no pair, he would possibly take a lot of cards, even a whole new hand, in an attempt to improve his holding. Remember, he earlier raised the pot (after first checking), so he was letting you know then that he probably had a more powerful hand than usual—in other words, a hand worthy of his raise.

That almost certainly means he has a hand stronger than one pair, but if he did have only one pair, such as...

why wouldn't he throw away the seven, four and eight. That way, he'd keep the pair of kings and have a chance of catching new cards which might make his hand even better. Maybe he could snag another king or a small pair or even two kings (making four kings!), three sixes (making a full house) or a king and a pair of nines (making an *even bigger* full house—kings full). Obviously, the old man would have virtually nothing to lose and much to gain by drawing cards to one pair.

If he had two pair, like...

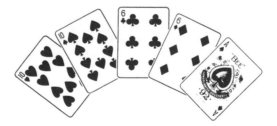

he could throw away the ace and hope to catch a ten or a six, making a full house. You could argue that he's likely to catch something smaller than the ace and end up with a slightly weaker hand than he started with, such as...

Sure, that's not quite as good as the original hand, but what's the difference? He still has the basic strength he started with—two pair, tens up over sixes. He still beats nines up (or worse) and still loses to jacks up (or better). So his only sacrifice would come in the very, very unlikely circumstance that you also finished with exactly two tens and two sixes. Even then, he has a good chance of winning by drawing a better hand than yours—either by snagging a higher extra card or by making a full house.

Usually, he would choose to draw to two pair. Similarly, if he held three of a kind, you'd expect him to draw two hoping to make four of a kind or a full house. If he failed, he'd still have the same three of a kind he began with and, in effect, the draw was a free bonus opportunity.

So what hand would you expect the old man to stand pat on? Certainly, a straight would be reasonable. He'd stand pat if he held this hand.

By now you should easily recognize that the hand shown is a straight. To qualify as a straight, remember, the five cards must be capable of being arranged from highest rank to the lowest rank with each succeeding card rating exactly one less in stature than the card before. Additionally, the cards must not be of the same suit, because that would make the hand among the most powerful in the poker universe—a straight flush. (Also, keep in mind that if cards consist of five, four, three, deuce and ace, the ace is construed as low and the hand can qualify as a straight or straight flush.)

The nine-high straight in the illustration probably didn't arrive in that easy-to-view order. It might have been this, instead.

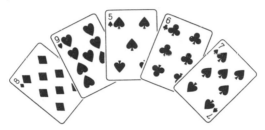

You should by now be able to recognize that just as easily. You do the arranging in your mind while leaving the poker hand in the same physical order as it was when you picked it up to look at it.

Now, then, why would the man draw any cards to a straight? He might throw away the five in hopes of catching a ten and making a higher straight: ten, nine, eight, seven, six. But common sense tells us that such a decision would be ludicrous. The odds would be heavily against making the better straight, and even if he succeeded, he wouldn't be much stronger than he was to begin with.

Hey, a straight is a very good hand. You should only expect one on the first five cards once in every 255 deals. You don't customarily draw when you have a complete straight already. Okay. Now it's clear. If the old man had a straight, that would be one reason why he'd choose to stand pat. What else could he hold? Maybe a flush. That's an even rarer hand which you'll get once every 509 hands on the average. If the old man had such good fortune, he'd surely stand pat. So, what else would be good to stand pat with?

This...

That's a full house. Typically, players do not throw away the one-pair part of a full house to draw to the remaining three of a kind. Sure, they might make four of a kind, but if they fail, they'd end up with just three of a kind. Sometimes, poker novices see that as an almost reasonable risk, but it isn't. The reason is this: It could happen quite frequently that you'd end up losing with three of a kind when you would have won had you stood pat on the full house. Conversely, there aren't many times that you'd win by making four of a kind when you would not also have won if you'd stood pat on the full house.

While this argument may seem to belabor the obvious, there is a very important concept at work here. And it applies both to poker and to everyday encounters (even though there are specific rare exceptions which are mathematically provable).

YOU SHOULD SELDOM JEOPARDIZE A HAND THAT'S PROBABLY GOING TO WIN IN THE HOPE OF MAKING AN EVEN BETTER HAND. YOU SHOULD SELDOM RISK A SUPERIOR BARGAINING POSITION IN ORDER TO GAIN AN EVEN BETTER POSITION.

The key words in the boxed paragraph are *jeopardize* and *risk*. I am certainly not telling you that it's wrong to gamble on gaining a more favorable hand in life or in poker. But I'm telling you to evaluate whether you're giving your opponent a better chance of winning by trying to improve your holding. Try to put yourself inside your opponent's mind and decide whether, if he knew what cards you were holding, he'd be hoping you'd draw. If he would want you to "draw" (whether at the poker table or elsewhere) because he had more hope of winning that way, then you definitely should *not* draw. Assuming that the old man knows instinctively what we've just discussed, he definitely won't draw to a full house. Since he's already chosen not to draw any cards, we must seriously consider the possibility that he holds a full house.

If he had a straight flush or a royal flush, it's obvious he would choose not to draw. What about four of a kind?

If he had...

would he be likely to draw? Yes! By throwing away the jack, he could keep the four of a kind, so he would have nothing to lose by drawing one card. However, he couldn't possibly improve the strength of his hand relative to your hand, so drawing a card seems futile. Well, it turns out that there is one basic advantage in drawing a card rather than rapping pat.

The advantage is that it will confuse you. If he were to draw one card to four of a kind, you might think, "The old man must have two pair." Yep. He would probably draw one card if he held four of a kind, because he's been around poker for many, many years and, if he's learned one important thing, it's this:

> ANYTIME IT DOESN'T COST ANYTHING TO CON-
> FUSE AN OPPONENT, YOU SHOULD DO IT. DON'T
> THINK ABOUT IT, IN LIFE OR IN POKER. YOU
> SHOULD AUTOMATICALLY ACCEPT ANY FREE
> OPPORTUNITY TO CONFUSE THE OPPOSITION.
> PERIOD.

Now, your first instinct might be to quarrel with the previous absolute statement. Your mind is possibly off on a mission of its own trying to find exceptions. You could probably conjure up a few, but if you examine them really objectively, you'll see that a confused opponent is always easier to destroy than a confident one. And this is triply true when you, as a woman, are involved in a conflict with a man.

I know, I know. You're saying to yourself that there might be some rare times when a confused man might be more dangerous than a secure man who understands his predicament. It so happens that this isn't true. Confused opponents can be easily overpowered if you follow through with the right winning moves. Confident opponents cannot be so easily overpowered. It *is* true that overconfidence makes your male opponent vulnerable, but total confusion makes him even more vulnerable, once you know how to take advantage.

So, confusion is a valuable tool for you. It is also a valuable tool for the old man, and he knows it. However, in order to confuse you by drawing one card to four of a kind, he must first *have* four of a kind. Fat chance! Players only get four of a kind once in 4,165 deals, on average. If he has a legitimate pat hand, it's overwhelming (more than 75 percent, likely) that he has either a straight flush or a flush. That would mean you'll most likely have a winner if you draw one card and make a full house.

But, back up a second! What does it mean: "a *legitimate* pat hand?" What other kind of pat hand is there? Could there be an illegitimate pat hand? You bet! Remember, when it's time to draw, every active player gets to choose how many cards he wants, if any. Players don't have to always draw the way that makes the most sense on the surface. They may try to confuse you. For instance, the old man might stand pat on two pair hoping that, if you have a better hand, you'll throw it away rather than call on the next round of betting. (That's right, there's another betting round coming up, so get ready!) Not only might he stand pat on two pair or some other medium-quality hand, but he might stand pat on nothing at all (no pair)!

Remember that he was not the opener, so he wasn't required to have a pair of jacks or better to play. Only the opener, Sonny in this hand, is required to have jacks or better. Anyone who subsequently enters the pot can have any hand they happen to fall in love with. Now, it's perfectly possible that the old man could have had no pair, checked and later raised as a bluff. You remember the concept of bluffing. Always consider, in poker and elsewhere, that your opponent could be bluffing. Certain players bluff more consistently than others.

So, you're not sure at this moment what the elderly man has, but it's more likely he has a legitimate pat hand than an illegitimate one. That's because good strategy dictates that deception should be used only occasionally, otherwise it fails to fool anyone, and experienced players, like this man, usually play straightforward poker. Let's say, for the moment, that we feel the man has a straight or a flush. Back to your hand. You hold two pair, aces and sevens with a three left over. The three isn't doing you any good, so you decide to discard it. Holding your cards carefully, to prevent anyone else from seeing them, you slide the unwanted card away from the other four cards and toss it facedown on the center of the table. Using one finger to indicate the number of cards you want, and you say, "Give me one please."

The dealer carefully takes the next card off the top of the deck and slides it across the table to you. Your cards won't necessarily be dealt to you this carefully, but here is a particularly cautious dealer who doesn't want to take any chances that someone else will see your card. That's poker courtesy at its finest, huh? Even before you reach for this new card, the old man has made a bet. The limit is $2 after the draw in this game. In some games, the limit after the draw is the same as it was before the draw, but that isn't the case here. Now it will cost you $2 more if you want to call. Otherwise, you'll have to throw away your hand and the old man will collect the pot, no matter what he has. Don't get mad! I know I didn't explain that when I coaxed you into calling, but I had other things on my mind.

What should you do now? First of all, look at your card and see if you helped your hand. Careful, peek but don't let anyone else see.

Look closely now. . .

Now put it with your other four cards and look at your final hand . . .

Suddenly, you've got the old man by the. . .well, anyway, you're the favorite!

Chapter Seven

Raking in the Money

It's time to raise. Raise, remember, means you're not only going to match the amount of money an opponent has bet, but you're going to put in *more* than he's bet.

To really understand the implications of a raise, you must keep in mind that (except in exceptional cases, discussed later, where players are short of chips and contending for a partial pot) all active players must have equal investments in the pot. Those not willing to match another player's investment, lose.

That's brutal, but that's the way with poker. It's also often the way with real life, as we'll see when we begin to scout the world around us to see where poker's being played without cards.

If a player has bet $1 and two other players have called, thereby each putting a matching $1 in the pot, then all three players, the original bettor and the two callers, remain eligible for the pot. If, however, either of the two callers had decided not to risk another $1, then that player would be out of contention for the pot and whatever money he or she had already invested would be lost forever. If no player calls, the bettor wins outright. At present, there are only two players, you and the old man. He bet $2, so you must call $2 to remain eligible. But why let this guy off easy? You've got sevens-full, for godsake! The man originally declined to bet with a pat hand, then raised after Sonny had opened and you had called. At that point, he was showing you no mercy. You drew a card and improved to a full house. That's a hand so powerful that it will destroy any straight or flush (the hands he's most likely to be holding), plus it will beat any full house smaller than your sevens-full.

Sounds good. Let's put the screws to him! "I raise," you announce. And you slide four white $1 chips into the pot. You did that perfectly. Many novices make the mistake of putting in the $2 to call the bettor, then returning to their stacks of chips to get the extra $2 with which to raise. That's called a *string bet* and it's usually illegal. Generally, it's okay to say, "I raise," before putting any chips in, then calling with some chips and going back for more. The stipulation is that you must say *raise* before you place any portion of the bet in the pot.

The rule against string bets is designed to keep players from doing the very thing you've seen in western movies. A player says, "I call your ranch . . . ," and here he pauses to gauge the reaction of his opponent who may already be exposing his hand . . . , "and I raise you three more ranches and a cow." Obviously, that isn't fair, because when the player calls, his foe thinks the betting is over and might either concede or grin gleefully. That's why, in most formal games of poker, you must declare your raise immediately when you act, or put in the full amount. You never call, pause, raise.

The way you did it was just right, and now the old man begins to tremble even more noticeably and gives you a hurt look. At this point, you have raised the investment required for him to continue playing. Either he must call $2 more or forfeit any right to compete for the pot. If he chooses to call, he'll get to see your hand, and you'll get to see his. There's only one round of betting before the draw and one round after. When this second betting round is completed, one player may have won by default (if no players were willing to match his or her investment) or all players with equal investments will show their hands so the winner can be determined according to the categories and subcategories of strength we've already discussed. That's how the winner will have

to be decided if the old man calls. There's one other possibility:
He could raise!

Sometimes there's a limit to the number of raises that can be
made in a single betting round. That limit, if there is one, is customarily three, four or five raises. After that last raise, the most
damage you can do to an opponent is to call. However, many
games have no limit on raises. In any case, there's no limit on
raises in this game, and anyway, that limit would not have been
reached yet, even if there were one. Besides that, there's seldom
a raising limit imposed when only two players remain in active
contention for the pot. The limit-on-raises rule is designed to prevent third parties from getting mixed up in a raising war between
two players. Anyway, none of that applies in this situation, but
I thought you should be aware of the possibilities when you sit
in your next poker game.

In response to your raise, the man slams $2 more in chips into
the pot and spreads his hand. "Is your flush bigger than mine?"
he wants to know.

You look at the hand which he has fanned face up on the table
in front of him . . .

"I don't have a flush," you say, your voice filled with imitation
sorrow.

"That's the breaks, lady," the old man grumbles, his voice
quavering only slightly. He reaches for the pot, beginning to scoop
it his way.

"But I do have a full house," you add. And you spread it face
up on the table in front of your stack of chips. You really shouldn't

do this. You've got to learn to show mercy when it's appropriate. Do whatever will help you win money, but don't badger the players without a specific motive. Many times, it pays to be popular. And while antagonism will work in your favor if used selectively, you should opt in favor of good humor any time you're in doubt.

Oh, what pain lives in the old man's face as he scans your cards! "Take the pot!" he chokes.

Be a diplomat now. Make things better. You smile, your eyes focused directly on his. You are sensitive to his pain, and you try to erase this feeling because this is poker which you've heard is akin to war. Don't fight your feeling of compassion! Dwell on it. Nurture it. Much of your success at poker and the arena beyond will come from feeling the hurt of others. It never, ever pays to make yourself insensitive to your surroundings. If there is glee, join it. If there is pain, feel it. However, you must act in your own best interests and not yield to your feelings. Sometimes, you must use an opponent's pain against him. That's the way the game goes. Don't let your empathy interfere with your drive for victory; but by all means, LET THERE BE EMPATHY.

Feel what others feel. Then act decisively on the information you discover and claim the rewards. Use every tool you can gather to build your victories. Don't ever let your goal grow misty with compassion. If you want to be generous, give the money back after you stack your chips. But focus first on winning; always focus on winning—first. Keep looking at the old man and don't stop smiling, even though he's presently avoiding your eyes. Now, you've got his attention. The pot is no longer being contended. This would be a good time to sweeten up to him. "Wow! That was a tough loss," you tell him. "I really got lucky to draw a seven. You had me beat from the beginning and then I just got lucky. I'm a very lucky person. You must be really upset with me."

His ego now bolstered, he smiles right back at you. "Hell, lady, I ain't upset. That's just poker. Maybe next time you'll have the flush and I'll get lucky. We don't take it personal around here."

Everyone nods their agreement. Then the man says, "Can I buy you a cup of coffee?"

"Well, Sonny just bought me one . . . but that was before all the delays and Sonny's speech and . . . sure, why not? Mine's probably cold by now." *How many cups of coffee do you get offered in a public poker room?* you wonder.

You stretch out your arms to gather the pot you've just won. Other players help by pushing the chips your way. Most of the time, you shouldn't worry about them handling the chips you've just won, because the majority of poker players are too honorable to palm any.

When you've got the pot near you in a haphazard pile, you begin to reorganize your chips. By the time you're finished, you have 16 white chips worth $1 each and 11 red chips worth a quarter each. You've got $18.75, already $8.75 more than what you started with. Suddenly you hear, "Let's deal the next hand." The voice rudely penetrates your euphoria, and strangely you recognize it as your own.

Chapter Eight

Opening Strategy

Every player eligible for the next poker pot begins by being dealt a hand. The hand may be initially very strong, such as the elderly man's pat flush. It may be moderately strong, such as your aces-up were before you made the full house. It may be of doubtful strength, such as a pair of jacks. It may be a hand of no apparent initial strength, such as this . . .

That's no pair, king high, and there aren't too many hands it could beat. But while its immediate strength is not very noteworthy, it's *potential* is awesome. Holy cow, gee whiz, think about it! Throw away that out-of-place seven of hearts, sort the hand mentally, and you'll be drawing one card to this . . .

You could catch a queen of clubs, make a king-high straight flush and be essentially unbeatable. Think about how proud you'd be. Any other club would give you a flush, almost certainly a winner and if you caught a queen of some other suit—diamonds, hearts or spades—you'd have a king-high straight. Even if you caught a second king, you'd have some small chance of winning.

When you have cards, like those, which have no real strength before the draw, but have a hot potential, you hold what's known as a *come hand*. If you play it, you're said to be *on the come*. Don't forget, there's a glossary of selected terms in the back of this book.

You might begin with a hand that has neither any current strength nor much realistic chance of improvement. Even in that case, you might win by bluffing if you're willing to risk the money.

This all leads us to one encompassing fact:

IN POKER, YOU WILL ALWAYS BE HOLDING SOME KIND OF HAND WHEN YOU ENTER A POT. IT MAY BE STRONG, WEAK OR MERELY FULL OF PROMISE. BEFORE YOU CAN PLAN A WINNING STRATEGY, YOU MUST FIRST LOOK AT YOUR CARDS AND ASSESS THEM.

IN DAILY LIFE, YOU WILL ALWAYS BE HOLDING SOME KIND OF *HAND* WHEN YOU ENTER A CONFRONTATION. IT, ALSO, MAY BE STRONG, WEAK OR MERELY FULL OF PROMISE. BEFORE YOU CAN PLAN A WINNING STRATEGY, YOU MUST FIRST LOOK AT THOSE REAL-LIFE *CARDS* AND ASSESS THEM.

Continuing now with your poker-specific training. let's look at the various hands you might hold in common situations and figure out how to play them for maximum profit.

Chapter Nine

What Hands to Play

In life and in poker, you always have a hand to play when the battle for the next pot begins. Many people make the mistake of looking at their hand and judging its worth relative only to the spectrum of other hands they might have been dealt. If it stands high on the ranking ladder, they like the hand. If it stands on a lower rung, they like it less. That's a terrible way to assess your power. Your primary strength or weakness is not governed by the cards you hold but, rather, by the cards you hold *relative to the probable cards of your opponents.*

Sometimes a pair of kings will be a profitable hand and sometimes it will be unworthy of investing a penny. One thing that is vital in assessing the relative strength of a poker hand is the number of opponents still to act behind you. If you're the very first player to decide whether to open a pot, you're in more jeopardy than if you're last. The reason is that when other players decline to open in front of you, it becomes less likely that they have any hand worth opening with. While it's true that players who check, thereby declining to open, *might* be sandbagging a powerful hand with the intention of later raising, it is more likely that they simply are not strong enough to open. Remember, sandbagging is an occasional tactic which wise players use selectively. They can't do it all the time, otherwise they'd lose their element of surprise. A player will check 100 percent of the time if he or she cannot open. But that player will often open if possible. For that reason, given the fact that an opponent has already checked, you should assume that he or she is less likely to hold openers than before the check was announced.

Here, let's try to see this more clearly. Suppose that you know your opponent will have a legal opening hand about 20 times out of 100. Gosh, that turns out to be close to the real probability. (You'll be dealt openers 20.63 percent of the time, if that statistic interests you.) If you don't know anything about your opponent's hand, then you must figure there's an 80 percent chance (80 hands out of 100) that he or she does not have openers and only a 20 percent chance (20 hands out of 100) to the contrary.

Now that's if you knew nothing about an opponent's hand. When that opponent checks, you *do* know something. Specifically, you know that the player, having all those rights and privileges afforded every poker player on earth, could have chosen to open if opening were legal. To be legal, remember, the hand would have to be at least as strong as a pair of jacks. Let's suppose that out of the 20 times that an opponent *could* open, he or she will actually open only 10 times on the average. This information would do you no good if the player hadn't acted yet. The hand would be unknown and would have an 80 percent chance of containing openers and a 20 percent chance of not containing them.

But suppose the opponent checked. Out of 100 hands, you could expect that opponent to check *every* time opening were illegal. That's 80 times. The opponent would have opened 10 of the 20 times that opening were legal (i.e. with a pair of jacks or stronger). The other 10 times he or she would have checked *with* openers.

So, the mathematical breakdown is this: When your opponent checks, there are only 10 chances out of 90 that he or she is checking with openers. Before he or she checks, there are 20 chances out of 100 (a far greater probability) that openers exist in that hand. The chance is 20 percent that the player has openers before checking; only 11 percent after checking.

What you've just learned is very hard to grasp for some people.

Keep thinking about it until you're certain you see why you're safer after players check than before.

We're dealing with a very important concept that says when an opponent has chosen not to take aggressive action, it's more likely than usual that his or her position is weak. That's not just poker talk; that's everywhere talk.

Even though the checking opponent could be disguising real strength, solid strategic theory must lead us to believe that this is less likely following the check than it was before.

Are there exceptions? Yes. There are a few players, for instance, who almost always check strong hands with the hope of later raising. Conversely, they tend to barge into pots with fairly weak hands. Such players will eventually destroy themselves using those tactics, because correct strategy dictates that poker must be played straightforward most of the time so that any tricky and exceptional moves will catch opponents by surprise. If you always opt for the surprises, then you are perceived to be treacherous and your strategies will seldom deceive.

The same is true in your everyday dealings. Your actions must *seem* straightforward enough to your opponents that they are willing to reply in the manner you expect them to. You can safely make them worry that you'll *occasionally* cross them up. But if you have implanted in their minds that your strategies are *always* suspect and there's something tricky about your every action, then you will be unable to maneuver your opponents the way you choose and your strategies will fail.

We know that when players have checked in front of us, it's less likely that they have openers than it was before they checked. The more players that check before it's your choice to open, the *less likely* it is that anyone has openers. That means, if you have openers, your hand is in less jeopardy depending on the number of opponents who have already checked.

But counting the players who have already checked is somewhat misleading. The really important consideration is how many new players (who have not yet acted on their hands) still must act behind you.

IN POKER OR IN LIFE, IF YOU DO NOT HAVE INFOR-
MATION ABOUT THE STRENGTH OF YOUR OPPONENTS'
HANDS, THE FIRST THING YOU SHOULD CONSIDER IS
HOW MANY PLAYERS REMAIN TO ACT BEHIND YOU. IF
THERE ARE MANY, YOU SHOULD USUALLY MAKE AN
OPENING BET WITH ONLY A STRONG HAND. IF THERE
ARE FEW, YOU MAY CHOOSE TO OPEN WITH FAR
WEAKER HANDS.

There is a second standard consideration in deciding whether or not to open. It is the size of the ante relative to the opening bet. Since, in the game you're playing, everyone puts a 25-cent ante in the pot before the cards are dealt, this constitutes the original prize that makes the hand worth winning. Without an ante, there would be little or no incentive to do battle.

In your game, the total of the antes is $2. The opening bet is a required $1; it can be no more or no less. Therefore the size of the cumulative ante relative to the opening bet is 2 to 1, or simply, the ante is twice as big as the opening bet. *The prize is twice the size of the investment.*

This turns out to be a liberal structure. By that, I mean that the ante is large enough in relation to the first bet (and the future bets) that it should stimulate action and encourage players to open, call and raise. An example of a more conservative structure would be the same 25-cent per player ante (for a $2 total), with an opening-bet requirement of $2. In such a game, the ante is no different, but the burden of the bet is twice as large. The ratio of prize vs. size of investment is 1 to 1 or even. In other words, you would bet the entire size of the pot to open, whereas in your game you can open by betting only half the size of the pot (and the prize is twice as large proportionately).

So . . .

IN POKER OR IN LIFE, IF YOU DO NOT HAVE IN-
FORMATION ABOUT THE STRENGTH OF YOUR OP-
PONENTS' HANDS, THE SECOND THING YOU
SHOULD CONSIDER IS HOW LARGE THE ANTE IS
RELATIVE TO THE OPENING BET. IF IT IS PROPOR-
TIONALLY LARGE, YOU MAY OPEN WITH
RELATIVELY WEAK HANDS. IF IT IS PROPOR-
TIONALLY SMALL, YOU MUST HAVE STRONGER
HANDS TO OPEN.

When you take both the number of players still to act and the size of the ante into consideration, you end up with these two tables which tell you which hands are generally appropriate to open with. Remember, you need at least a pair of jacks to be eligible to open.

TABLE A

MINIMUM PROFITABLE OPENERS
(ANTES TOTAL $2 AND BET IS $2)

(Any hand three of a kind or stronger is profitable
to open with in any position.)

PLAYERS TO ACT

7	Pair of aces, two pair *higher than* queens-up, one-card draw to flush which includes opening pair of jacks, queens or kings.

6	Pair of aces, two pair *higher than* queens-up, one-card draw to flush which includes opening pair of jacks, queens or kings.
5	Pair of kings or aces, two pair *higher than* jacks-up, one-card draw to flush which includes opening pair of jacks, queens or kings.
4	Pair of kings or aces, two pair *higher than* nines-up, one-card draw to flush which includes opening pair of jacks or queens.
3	Pair of queens or higher, any two pair, one-card draw to flush which includes opening pair of jacks, one-card draw to straight open at both ends which includes opening pair of jacks.
2	Any openers except a pair of jacks, one-card draw to flush which includes opening pair of jacks, one-card draw to straight open at both ends which includes opening pair of jacks.
1	Any openers.

Notice how your requirements to open the pot profitably diminish as there are fewer players behind you who haven't yet acted on their hands. If you aren't quite clear about what the table means, don't worry. I'll provide examples shortly. First, compare the previous table (intended for eight players anteing 25-cents each when the opening bet is $1) with the next table (where the ante is still 25 cents per player but the opening bet is $2).

TABLE B

MINIMUM PROFITABLE OPENERS
(ANTES TOTAL $2 AND BET IS $1)

(Any hand three of a kind or stronger is profitable to
open with in any position.)

PLAYERS TO ACT

7	Pair of aces, two pair *higher than* jacks-up, one-card draw to flush which includes opening pair of jacks, queens or kings.
6	Pair of aces, two pair *higher than* nines-up, one-card draw to flush which includes opening pair of jacks, queens or kings.
5	Pair of kings or aces, two pair *higher than* nines-up, one-card draw to flush which includes opening pair of jacks or queens.
4	Pair of queens or higher, any two pair, one-card draw to flush which includes opening pair of jacks, one-card draw to straight open at both ends which includes opening pair of jacks.
3	Any openers except a pair of jacks, one-card draw to flush which includes opening pair of jacks, one-card draw to straight open at both ends which includes opening pair of jacks.

| 2 | Any openers. |
| 1 | Any openers. |

Notice that sometimes the requirements stay the same from position to position. That's no misprint. The opening requirements for the two tables were carefully selected. From time to time, you may alter them to suit the pace of your game and the nature of your opponents. But be careful. Don't stray very far from these proven standards. You should also keep in mind that the suggested openers are not absolute. If a table suggests that you *may* open with a particular hand, that does not mean you *must* open.

Notice how much less liberally you can open with the $2 opening bet than with the $1 opening bet. That's because, WHEN YOU MUST RISK MORE MONEY, YOU REQUIRE MORE STRENGTH.

It may bother you that you're sometimes allowed to open with a pair of aces, but not allowed to open with two small pair, which rank higher. That's because one pair is easier to improve by drawing; and that's a concept you'll want to keep in mind when you play.

Just so you understand the tables, here are some examples of what's a recommended opening hand and what isn't. In fact, let's make this a quiz so we can be completely certain you know which hands to open with.

Suppose you have this hand . . .

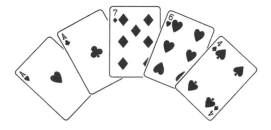

You are playing the $2-to-open game. There are six players left to act behind you (which means, in an eight-handed game, that the first player has already checked). Is it profitable to open?

You should have answered yes. In fact, in both tables of opening requirements, it's always profitable to open with aces.

You are playing in your $1-to-open game with seven players still to act. This means you're the first player to make a decision. Here's your hand . . .

Should you open? Yes, but barely. The table demands that any two pair you open with be *higher than* jacks up. Therefore, you would not normally have opened with . . .

What about the $2 game? Is this hand strong enough to open with if there are seven players to act behind you . . .

Sorry, that hand is too weak.

How about this one in your $1-to-open game with four players still to act behind you . . .

Would you open? You should say no, but it's close. You require a pair of queens here. (For technical reasons, the fact that the hand contains an ace and a queen makes it safer to open, but we won't deal deeply with that. The simple explanation is that the ace and the queen limit the possible pairs of those ranks opponents could have and, thereby, make it somewhat less likely that you'll be beaten.)

Same $1-to-open game. With three players who haven't yet acted behind you, should you open with this hand . . .

Yes! Even though that's only a pair of jacks, it has a secondary strength. You could throw away the jack of diamonds and draw one card to a heart flush. If you missed, you'd lose, but if you connected with another heart you could claim a major pot! Throwing away one of your opening jacks to draw to a straight or a flush is called *splitting openers*. A common rule is that you must show your discarded jack and announce that you're splitting openers. This indicates to the other players that you had legal openers to begin with and did not open falsely. Normally, you would split only if you were raised and then called the raise. However, this extra advantage of being able to split openers if you must, is enough to make the pair of jacks playable when it otherwise would not have been.

Here's another hand ...

You're in the $2-to-open, 25-cent ante game with two players behind you who haven't acted. Do you open? Yes, because you can draw to a straight open at both ends. In this case, the potential straight is made up of queen-jack-ten-nine and needs an eight or a king to complete it. Since there are four eights and four kings in a standard deck, there are eight cards which could make this straight. That's why it's known as an *eight-way* straight attempt.

The table allows you to play that hand. Keep in mind, though, that the example below is not an open-ended, eight-way straight...

because, if you threw away a jack, you'd have only one rank of card to make a straight. Specifically, you'd need to catch a ten. Since there are only four tens in the deck, this is known as a *four-way* straight attempt or, even more commonly, an *inside* straight attempt. Inside straight tries are not profitable. Even coupled with an opening pair, they aren't of much use. That's because, if you opened and were faced with a raise, you'd generally be better off drawing three to the pair than one to the inside straight.

Study the tables until you have a good feel for the appropriate opening hands. As you can see, the second table (where the bet is smaller relative to the antes) lets you open more liberally. That's the game you're now playing. (Would I seat you in a game where you couldn't play lots of hands?)

On both tables, you always have the option to open if you have three of a kind or better. Also, you can open whenever you can split a pair of jacks or better and draw one to a straight flush (pretty rare).

That will give you an idea of which hands you should open with. Some pots are not opened by anyone. Then the antes stay in the pot and, in your game, you add another ante. But more than 80 percent of all pots *will* normally be opened. The strategy you use to open pots is a bit more conservative (and a bit more profitable) than that used by your opponents. For this reason, of every 12 pots that are opened at your table, *you* will only open one of them on the average. Fortunately, there are ways to enter a pot besides opening. Let's look at them now.

Chapter Ten

Getting Involved

You must understand that when you hold weak or moderate hands ... IT'S USUALLY BETTER TO LET SOMEONE ELSE OPEN THE POT THAN TO OPEN IT YOURSELF. Once you're happy with this concept, you'll find many daily circumstances where you can use it to your own gain.

If you elect to open, then you're already involved. If you elect to check, you may be hoping that nobody will open (and that way your ante will remain in the pot for the next hand which you may win) or you may be hoping someone else opens so you can call or raise.

Essentially, there are only two ways to get involved:
1. Starting the war yourself by opening;
2. Letting someone else start the war.

EVERY HAND, IN POKER AND IN LIFE, GIVES YOU THE CHOICE OF GETTING INVOLVED OR NOT GETTING INVOLVED.

As one of my top female students wrote in a required report, "Once the commitment is made, the follow-through is easy. It's the initial decision to act or not act that requires much analysis. Should you get involved—with a man, with a project, with a career, with a hand? After all, another one is bound to come along which just might be better than the one you have now. So do you or don't you?"

The bottom line is that you must play ONLY THOSE HANDS WHICH ARE IN YOUR BEST INTEREST. Here are two examples of hands you could play if someone else opened the pot . . .

* * * Example One * * *

The complexion of your game has changed. Public poker is not like private home poker where the same players usually remain for a whole playing session. In public games, the players come and go. In this case, all the original players have left the game during the past one and a half hours, some to play bigger games and some to go home.

You're particularly distressed that your friend, the businessman who was seated to your right went broke and left the game. You can still almost feel his pain, even though he tried to smile politely when he rose to leave, declaring, "That's it for me. It's been nice playing with you."

You have opted to play conservatively and haven't entered in a single pot since winning with the full house. That's called "tight" poker. Tight means conservative, and not playing even one hand in an hour and a half is very, very tight. Too tight. Try to find a few hands to play, just to keep your opponents aware of your presence. Raise and stand pat. It's easier for women to get away with this occasionally than men. Loose means liberal.

There are seven players in the game, which means there's a seat open. (A full draw-poker game consists of eight players.) The seating arrangement looks like this . . .

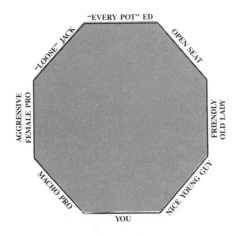

You'd be doing me a favor if you studied that diagram for a minute or so. Look where you're sitting. You have a Nice Young Guy on your right and a Macho Pro left.

You must keep in mind that there are two types of players you'd prefer to have on your *right*, so you can usually act *after* they act. Type one is a very aggressive or tricky player who is dangerous if allowed to play on your left. It doesn't matter if you're better or if you feel you "know how to handle" that player. If you allow aggressive, knowledgeable players to exist for a long time at your left, they will eat into your profits. Even if your skills are vastly superior to theirs, remember that you are not in a position to punish players on your left as consistently or severely as players on your right.

If you were to total all the poker profit you earned in your lifetime, you'd find that most of it came from players seated to your right. When I deal with this subject at poker seminars, many professional players are surprised when I present evidence that, over their poker careers, they *lose money* to players on their left. EVEN THE BEST PLAYER IN THE WORLD WILL LOSE MONEY FOR LIFE TO RELATIVELY STRONG PLAYERS SEATED

TO THE LEFT. That's why you should always be conscious of your seating position.

IN LIFE BEYOND POKER, YOU WILL LOSE GROUND TO STRONG ADVERSARIES WHO ACT AFTER YOU DO. YOU WILL GAIN GROUND BY PULVERIZING OPPONENTS WHO ACT BEFORE YOU DO. THAT IS THE LAW OF POKER. THAT IS THE LAW OF EVERYDAY ENCOUNTERS. THAT IS MY LAW. THE BEST YOU CAN HOPE TO DO IS NEUTRALIZE STRONG OPPONENTS WHO ACT AFTER YOU OR EARN SMALL PROFITS FROM WEAK OPPONENTS WHO ACT AFTER YOU. YOU WILL EARN BIG PROFITS FROM EVERYONE WHO ACTS BEFORE YOU. SUCH IS THE IMPORTANCE OF POSITION.

Obviously, someone has to act first and someone has to act second. If there are only two persons involved, you and an adversary, it is almost always to your advantage to try to be second.

When many players are involved in a poker game, here are some rules to help you to decide where to sit:

1. Both loose players and threatening players belong on your right. You want to act after these, as you've already learned.

2. Players who pose little or no threat and tight players belong on your left, also as you've already learned.

3. If there is a choice between sitting behind (so that the player is on your right and acts first) a skilled, aggressive man and a skilled, aggressive woman, then the skilled aggressive *woman* must go on your right. This is so important, it makes me tremble just to think about it. YOU MUST BE THE QUEEN OF YOUR GAME. Allowing another woman to

have a better position means that *she* and not you will reap most of the benefits of male-vs.-female ego wars. In life, it's even more important that you be THE LAST WOMAN TO ACT! If you are perceived as sexy or cute, you might try to steal the "queen of the table" image from other contenders by flirting or being coy. Feel your way. If you are perceived as matronly or just "one of the boys," let someone else do the flirting and promote an image of power. Whatever it takes to be "queen"—do it.

4. Men who are easy to pacify by befriending or flirting and men who will give up easily if bullied by a woman belong on your left. You can safely let these guys act behind you because you can maneuver them into posing no particular threat.

REMEMBER THE POLITICS OF POSITION: USUALLY BEFRIEND THOSE WHO ACT LAST. USUALLY ATTACK THOSE WHO ACT FIRST.

When you think about it, it's pretty clear that you should grab the open seat before someone else does. So, announce that you're changing seats and slide your chips over. By the way, you only have $5.75 remaining, since you've done nothing but ante quarters for the last hour and a half. Whoops! You've giving the impression that you're changing seats for tactical reasons. Wash that proud look off your face. Whenever you change positions, in poker or in life, make sure your opponents think you're doing this for incidental or even superstitious reasons. There's no sense letting your opponents know that you're improving your situation. That will make them more cautious and defensive.

Say something. "I think I'll try that seat over there. I haven't picked up a hand in over an hour. I think my luck will be better in a different seat."

That was very good! I liked the way you phrased it. Now your position looks like this . . .

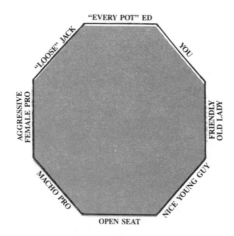

Much better! "Every Pot" Ed, who can't throw any hands away for a single bet, will act first. He'll commit himself to a lot of pots with small pairs or worse. You may even find him drawing two cards to hands like this . . .

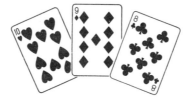

in a desperate attempt to snare a pot. Occasionally he'll win, but the effort will cost him so much that he'll have almost no chance of cashing out any chips. Figure him to go busted, and it's better you get the money than someone else. The style I'm going to teach you shortly is very dynamic. All the world-class players are selective about which hands they play, but once they involve themselves in a pot, they play very aggressively. When you're through exploring poker and begin practicing it as a science, you'll be playing at or near a world-class level, so it's important to keep the solid-but-aggressive image in mind.

Anyway, when you play aggressively, you do more than your share of raising. Although compulsively loose players such as Ed will enter pots for one bet almost every chance they get, they do have some reservations about calling raises. They may *call* that $1 bet with . . .

or . . .

but they won't usually call a bet and a raise ($2) to come in cold. Suppose the pot has been opened and you have . . .

Your loose opponent has ...

If he acts before you, he'll call, you'll raise and, now that he already has $1 invested and it only costs him another $1, he'll probably call that extra $1, too. You'll trap him for $2. But if you act first, you'll raise the opener and the loose player with two eights is going to figure that (as much as it hurts to throw a hand away) he's not willing to invest $2 to call the raise without having anything invested.

Ed's on your right now, and that's where you want him. Also on your right is "Loose" Jack, an "Every Pot" Ed clone. So, again, he's in a good spot, since both he and Ed usually will be acting before you. The Macho Professional and the Aggressive Female Professional are both types you also want on your right. While you weren't able to accomplish this perfectly by switching seats, you certainly did improve your situation by getting them away from your immediate left where they could do the most damage.

Friendly Old Lady and Nice Young Guy are both people who

play their cards pretty routinely and never give you many troubles or surprises. Since they can neither provide much easy money or cause you much trouble, they're perfect candidates to sit to your left and act behind you.

All in all, you've made a very good seat change, lady!

Anyway, some of you will remember that this is Example One of hands you can get involved with when you are not the opener. Maybe I got sidetracked, but I didn't forget.

Aggressive Female Pro has just dealt the cards and suddenly Macho Pro barks, "Open!" Loose Jack calls the dollar and so does Every Pot Ed. You look at your hand, and it is this . . .

What should you do? That's right, raise! Three kings is a very strong hand, and you can even improve it on the draw. It's unlikely that Macho Pro opened with anything better. Knowing his character, you suppose that if he did have a stronger hand, it would be very likely that he'd check and try to raise later. Macho Pro sandbags more often than he should because it strokes his ego. Either Jack or Ed would probably have raised with so much as aces-up or three of a kind. So you probably have the best hand.

"I raise!" I like the way you said it. Your tone of voice was almost playful.

Everyone passes through Aggressive Female Pro, the dealer. Macho Pro, the opener, thinks and thinks. Statistically, the most probable thing he has is a pair of aces. If he does, the odds are almost 7 to 1 against him making at least three aces. Even then, he wouldn't necessarily beat your three kings, because you could improve to a full house. All in all, if he had two aces and knew

107

you had three kings, he'd need less than 6 to 1 for his money to make calling your raise worthwhile. That's because he would generally expect to gain some ground after the draw if he made three aces, for instance by betting and being called. These concepts are difficult and if you understand them vaguely, that's good enough. Since both Ed and Jack figure to call and there's $2 in antes to begin with, Macho Pro will be getting 9 to 1 for his money if he calls. The $9 consists of $2 from each of three opponents, plus his opening $1 bet, plus the $2 in antes.

Clearly, it's to his advantage to call. Which brings us to another great rule of poker and beyond.

---

1. WHEN IT'S TO AN OPPONENT'S ADVANTAGE TO PLAY, IT'S USUALLY TO YOUR ADVANTAGE THAT HE OR SHE PASSES; AND . . .

2. WHEN IT'S TO AN OPPONENT'S ADVANTAGE TO PASS, IT'S USUALLY TO YOUR ADVANTAGE THAT HE OR SHE CALLS.

Looking at statement #1, the concept is that the theoretical profit going to an opponent must come from somewhere, and if you're figuring on winning the pot, a share of that opposing profit comes from you. It's been fashionable among some authorities to state it's always to your disadvantage to have any opponent in your pot who's earning a theoretical profit. That last reasoning is wrong.

Just imagine that there was an eight-handed game and six players had already called with pat straights. That's highly unlikely, but this is just intended to demonstrate a point which is easier to grasp in its extreme case. You call drawing to a big ace-high flush. The opponent next to you considers calling with a smaller jack-high flush draw. It's to his advantage to call because the odds are only about 4 to 1 against (4.22 to 1 to be exact, varying slightly depending on the circumstances) him making it and he'll get 9 to 1 (seven opponents at $1 each plus a $2 ante) for his money if he makes the flush and wins.

So this is a profitable play for your opponent, but it is *not* unprofitable for you, because if you make your big flush, you'll still win the pot even if he makes his flush. In fact, you'll win more when you include his $1 in the winnings. So, contrary to what other authorities may teach, there are cases when it is to both your advantage and your opponent's advantage for him to play.

In any case, you now have raised with three kings and it would be to your advantage if Macho Pro passed. This is not one of those rare situations in which it is to both of your advantages for him to call. It is to his advantage only.

At the moment, he's hesitating. How can you make him pass? Well, here's a really important concept: *Do nothing*. Whenever you want a player not to act, whether at poker or in business, do nothing unless there is an overpowering and obvious strategy that will cause him or her to "pass." The reason is simple. Players come to a poker table to gamble. They want reasons to call, and anything you do might trip their call mechanisms. They are more likely to pass if you do nothing. Tapping your fingers may lure a call. Smiling may lure a call. Glaring may summon their ego and lure a call. Away from the poker table the same is true. Most people are looking for reasons to get involved and profit.

---

1. IT'S USUALLY BETTER TO TAKE NO ACTION THAN TO TRY RANDOM STRATEGIES TO GET A PLAYER TO PASS; AND ...

2. IT'S USUALLY BETTER TO DO ANYTHING THAN TO JUST WAIT IN HOPES THAT A PLAYER WILL CALL.

Right now you're sitting passively hoping Macho Pro will pass. He just did! Good work.

Instantly, Loose Jack and Every Pot Ed call your raise. They draw three cards each. You draw two, not helping your three kings.

It's the opener who acts first after the draw, but when the opener is no longer involved in the pot, the first option passes to the left (clockwise). Jack bets! And Ed calls! Is this good for you or bad for you? Could they have made better hands than your three kings? Possibly, but it's much more likely that they made two pair or three of a kind. Since neither of them was the opener and since they both play small pairs almost routinely, there's a good chance they started with pairs smaller than your kings. If that is so, then even if they made three of a kind, you'd still have the winning hand.

"I raise!" you announce, calling the $2 bet and adding $1.50 more. A normal required raise is $2, but since you only had $1.50 left in front of you, that became the appropriate raise. They both call and you win. Your profit on the pot was $14 and you now have $19.50, almost twice what you started with. Poker is simple, huh?

* * * Example Two * * *

Another example of a hand you could play profitably without being the opener is this . . .

Since a pair of jacks or some better hand is required to open, you can't legally put in the first bet. However, it is frequently in your best interests to call with this hand and draw one card to the flush.

Rather than list example after example of hands that you can play without opening, I think you're ready for some serious learning. While the next crash courses in different forms of poker are simpler than the advanced material I present in other books and seminars, they will give you a good foundation.

All of these were published in a more consise form in *Gambling Times* magazine. Here, they have been slightly modified to include advantages you have as a woman. Specific advice has been added about male-female ego wars and how to capitalize on them. All in all, you'll find these slightly more aggressive in many areas than the strategies I have made available to a general male and female audience. Let's take a look.

PHOTO GALLERY

CECELIA "CISSY" RUSSO

"Poker is just a game and it is a game that men can play as well as women. The men I find easy to dominate are those who resent the fact that I, as a woman, am a good poker player."

When David Sklansky rated the best women poker players (*POKER PLAYER* 1/9/84) there was no doubt in his mind that "...she is in a class by herself so far as the rankings are concerned." Her game is limit hold 'em and she prefers to concentrate on the $10-$20 games around Las Vegas which she considers the "juiciest." Russo relies heavily on her instincts for making the right decisions while playing, and she sometimes consults outside authorities on poker theory. She believes that a quality known as "gamesmanship" makes a good card player—that and DISCIPLINE.

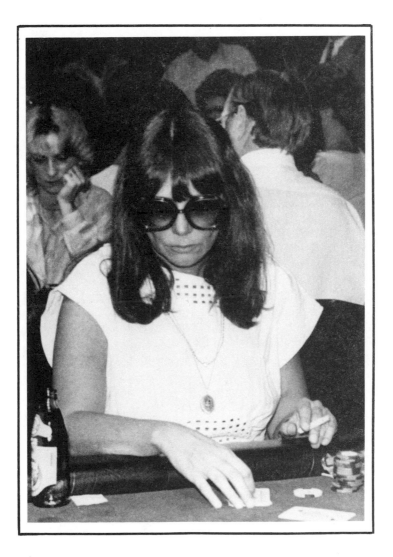

WANDA SANTORI

"When playing poker, my strategy is to play people rather than men or women."

Wanda Santori is a familiar face to most poker pros. She is one of the few women shift bosses in the industry and works all the major tournaments. During her nine years in Las Vegas, Santori played all limits of seven-stud. Now she is content to play small-limit poker for enjoyment. "I love the game and most of the people involved in the game. I hope I'm around poker forever."

SANDY STUPAK

"I admit I'm still a bit intimidated by high stakes poker, but I love to play with the best. I've noticed that the better the player is the more of a gentleman he is as well."

Sandy Stupak, wife of Vegas World owner Bob Stupak, has only been playing poker for a year and a half, and she admits she only learned out of desperation. It seems that Bob spends most of his spare time playing and Sandy was bored. She, nevertheless, shocked the poker community with her outstanding performance at the 1984 World Series of Poker. First, she won a $10,000 buy-in to the World Series of Poker main event by matching wits with some of poker's top pros, including George Huber and "Austin Squatty"—and coming out on top. She then went on to claim victory in the Casino Operators' Tournament, beating many seasoned veterans of the game.

CYNDY VIOLETTE

"I'd much rather play poker with men because they don't give women credit for knowing anything. I find that when their egos are involved in beating me, they'll just about chase me down with anything."

At age 24, Cyndy Violette's youthful appearance makes her look vulnerable at the poker tables and she invariably uses it to her advantage. She was one of three women who entered the championship no-limit hold 'em tournament at the 1984 World Series of Poker and she did it by winning the Palace Station satellite for that event. In that satellite, she spent six grueling hours playing heads-up poker against her only remaining opponent before claiming victory and the $10,000 buy-in. She says she's constantly improving her game by playing and learning from better players as she moves up in class.

SHELLEY CARR

"Being a woman poker player is good for a few extra bets a night. A man will call me more often than he would call another man in the same situation."

Shelley Carr is regarded by her friends and peers as one of the best low-limit poker players in the Las Vegas community. In 1983, she won a satellite sponsored by the Bingo Palace (now known as the Palace Station) where she deals poker professionally, and represented them in the mixed doubles tournament at the Horseshoe's World Series of Poker. Although Carr's skill is sufficient for her to move up to higher limits, she seems content to remain a recreational player for the time being.

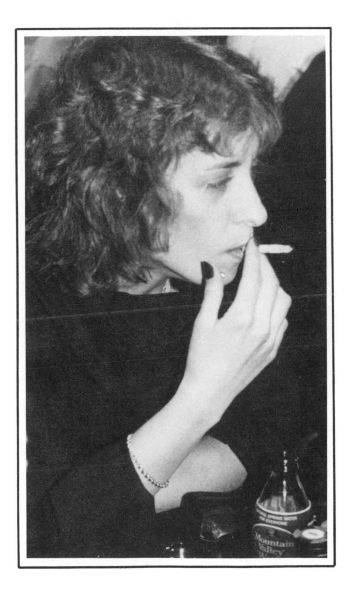

JOY SPENO

"I always remain cool and calm at the poker table, no matter what transpires . . . then, I go up to my room and scream."

You can see Joy at every major poker tournament held in Nevada. At the 1983 World Series of Poker she came in fifth in the Women's event. At poker she likes to gamble with the best and always seems to have the chips. She claims her skill comes from experience. Back home in upstate New York, she works hard as an accountant and found that coming out to Las Vegas helped her relax. When her luck turned sour at the blackjack tables she turned to poker and hasn't doubled down since.

TERRY KING

"I am able to bluff more because I'm a woman. They (the men) don't seem to expect it and I use that to my advantage."

When Terry King was still dealing poker for a living, she entered and won the 1978 Women's Stud Tournament at Binion's Horseshoe. She has never looked back since and has gone on to win the money and the respect of her male counterparts. Noted poker authority, David Sklansky (*POKER PLAYER* 12/12/83), included King in his list of best all-around players. She was the only woman named. When rating the best women players (*POKER PLAYER* 1/9/84), Sklansky added . . . "she plays quite a few games well and has held her own against some of the best players in the world."

D. MEYERSON

"The majority of poker players are men. And I'm glad. Because when I sit down in a game most of the men are going to give me their money."

D. Meyerson, a native of Oregon, has made Nevada her home for the past seven years. She is multi-talented; successful as a photographic artist as well as a psychotherapist. With her busy schedule, she still finds time to frequent the local Las Vegas cardrooms where she specializes in seven-stud and participates in weekly tournaments to enhance her skills. She has made winning a habit.

JUNE W. FIELD

"Remain sympathetic with a male player if he loses a big hand to another player. This will tend to make him more protective toward you."

Each year the World Series of Poker sponsors an all-women seven-stud event. In 1982, June Field walked away with all the chips and claimed $16,000 in prize money by eliminating all 63 other competitors. Today, she continues as a top competitor, participating in the many tournaments held in and around Las Vegas. Field also shares her experience and expertise in the game by contributing many informative and entertaining articles to *POKER PLAYER* newspaper, the leading publication for the poker industry.

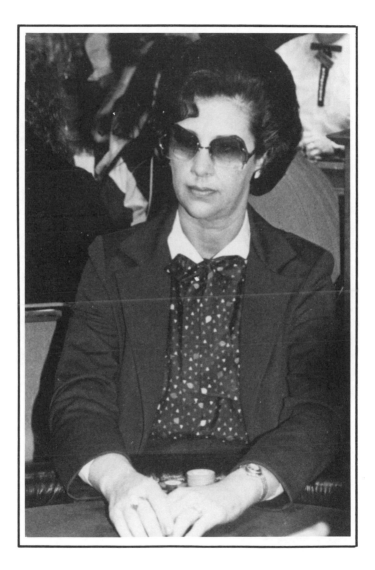

ERMA HART

"The majority of male players immediately perceive a female player as synonymous with 'live one.' How do I utilize their perceptions to my maximum advantage within the poker arena? Well, I'll take the fifth."

Born and raised in Brooklyn, New York, Erma Hart relocated to California in 1978 after graduating from Brooklyn College. She accepted a position as a consumer sales representative. Between calling on accounts in and around Los Angeles, she would investigate Gardena's legal poker clubs. By 1980, Hart was playing cards full time. She is considered by many authorities to be among the top ten women players alive.

Chapter Eleven

Five-Card Draw:
A Crash Course for Women

Since I'm changing these crash courses around and enhancing them to fit a female audience, I have some hard choices to make. For instance, should I leave the lead-ins that appeared in the original form. Particularly, should I leave the one that precedes *this* crash course in five draw. It can easily be construed as somewhat sexist, even though my intentions are pure.

I just keep blurting out things that offend some women. It's my favorite talent. There's really nothing I can do about it, even if I wanted to. I hold nothing but love and fairness in my heart. Why the lead-in to this crash course annoyed so many women, I'm not precisely sure. But in order to keep calm between me and those few sensitive readers, I've decided to delete ... I'm prepared to edit ... I'll cut out the offending ... Ah, hell! Here it is, almost exactly the way I wrote it. The magazine is *Gambling Times* and my monthly column is called *Caro on Gambling*. Are you ready?

Look, I didn't want to write about draw poker this month. I've got other stuff on my mind.

Here's an example. A month ago I was at a party and this medium-young woman said, "Poker? I could never play poker. I don't believe in competition."

So I asked (these weren't my exact words, but they're as close as I can remember), "Okay, medium-young woman, tell me why you don't like competition."

"Because I believe in cooperation."

Didn't that nonsense die out five or six years ago? Guess not. For a while, people were teaching their kids not to compete. Games faded from fashion. Too bad. Nobody gets very good at anything that way. You see, competition is an agreed upon endeavor. The result is that everyone grows stronger!

Competition and cooperation are not opposites. They are both powerful concepts, but they exist in harmony. There *is* no competition without cooperation.

This subject isn't meaningless and abstract. It is of particular importance to gamblers.

But now, I've got to keep my promise. I said this would be about five-card draw poker. Elementary ethics dictate that I deliver.

You are forbidden to take this course until you understand the following:

This is *not* a discussion of sophisticated techniques. Complicated plays, ploys and probabilities have been omitted. These guidelines have been smoothed out—that is, the advice has been tailored to fit a wide range of situations in a highly profitable way. There are situations where use of this advice will be wrong, but, even so, if you stubbornly use this method without variation, you *must* win in the small-limit game for which it is intended.

So far in this book, I've had you playing small-limit poker. That's because, it's best to familiarize yourself with the game at that level. I fully expect you to use some of these concepts to destroy male opponents in big-limit poker and in the big-limit, real-life world around you.

When I teach advanced tactics to men, I put a great deal of emphasis on involved tactical considerations. We use a lot of mathematical and logical strategic analysis. Many women who have followed my more general poker teachings, will see that I'm using a slightly different approach in this book. That's because, in a man-vs-man environment, once you've mastered the basics, the main gains are in improving your advanced strategy.

When I teach advanced tactics to women, I advise them to learn advanced strategy as extra icing. Mainly though, intelligent women will prosper because men can be battered about so easily in the face of a knowledgeable, aggressive woman. Many men will self-destruct and give you their money rather than face having to lose in a contest where they put forth their best effort.

Your best course is to learn the basics as presented here and remember that you *are* a woman. Being a woman in a sexist environment heavy with male ego is an advantage. When you play your cards right (which, by itself, surprises many men) and attack rather than sit back timidly, men will give you money in many ways, as you'll quickly learn just by sitting at the poker table.

What's the purpose of these quick courses? To teach intelligent women some easy-to-understand standards which can be learned quickly.

No attempt is made to provide advice for everything you might encounter in a poker game. What if you make a very high flush and the opener, who stood pat, bets into you—call or raise? When should you bet three of a kind into a three-card draw? How many raises should you go with a pat straight-flush?

Answers to questions such as these are not supplied. The presumption is that you'll use your own best judgment and that it will be at least equal to the judgment of your unsophisticated opponents. Sometimes you'll make the wrong play, but so will they. It evens out.

You will win because the advice given is, in itself, enough to snare mountains of chips against weak-to-moderate opposition— particularly against men who don't know how to handle a woman who plays more forcefully than they do.

Although many of the guidelines you're about to learn work well for home games, and they're even useful for a 52-card deck without a joker, this discussion deals with the game as it's played legally in California and by convention throughout most of America. Draw poker has been legal in Gardena, in the Los Angeles area for almost 50 years. The clubs are clean, lavish and public and they cater to women customers. The same is true in nearby Bell, Bell Gardens and Commerce. Many card clubs prosper in San Diego and Northern California.

The newest, largest and plushest poker club in the world is the Bicycle Club, which opened in November, 1984. It's in Los Angeles County, a few minutes from downtown, and a heavy emphasis is placed on attracting female poker players to its 120 tables.

Most of the California clubs operate 24 hours a day, offer security and set high standards for the rest of the nation. While Las Vegas is also a good place for poker, the game of draw is seldom played there.

To be sure, there are large and small cardrooms throughout California—all devoted to five-card draw poker (either standard or lowball) and all legal. But Gardena, Bell, Bell Gardens, Commerce and Huntington Park (all in the same Los Angeles area) spell poker paradise.

Legislation is underway to legalize other forms of poker in California. This will be a good place to live or visit if you plan on earning your living playing hold 'em or seven stud. More on those games later.

Our target game for this course is $2/$4 limit draw poker. You can walk right in and sit down at this game. Using the formula that comes next, you'll begin making money immediately. Later, you'll be able to add your own strategies and finesses.

A friend who's written a poker book once confided, "You can't just take someone off the street and teach him to beat draw poker."

Sounds reasonable, John. But I can. And here is that formula.

---

* * * Rules * * *

First let's get the rules straight. There are eight players per table. Each deals in turn. The ante is 25 cents. Before the draw all bets are $2. A pair of jacks or better is required to open. You can draw as many cards as you wish, up to five. After the draw, all bets and raises are $4. Occasionally no one will open. Then there's another quarter ante and the stakes become $3 before the draw and $6 after. If the pot still isn't opened, a third quarter is anted, making the total 75 cents per player, and the betting becomes $4/$8.

Got it?

Choose a table. The best is one where there are a lot of players per pot and everyone seems to be having a good time. Find a table full of males, particularly ones that look like they could be pushed around. The best indication (though occasionally wrong) are those in business suits and ties. Try to find a table without a woman who might compete with you for attention.

Look at your first hand. Remember, it takes jacks or better to open. Your hands will only be that good 22.4 percent of the time.

(I'll be referring to seating POSITION throughout this text. The player immediately to the left of the dealer has a position rating of seven, because that's how many players still must act behind him or her. To the left of position seven is position six, and so forth. The dealer has a position rating of zero. The order of action is clockwise.)

Okay, you're only going to get openers about twice in nine deals. Suppose you're in first position (position rating: 7) with this hand . . .

Not only do you have openers, but you hold a pair considerably better than plain old jacks. In fact, you'll only get a hand this good about one time in six. Your pulse rises. You clear your throat. Excitedly, your hands reach for your chips as you prepare to open. DON'T DO IT!

Are you nuts? You can't open with kings in first position! Remember the game you learned earlier in the book. That, too, was five-card draw, but there's one huge difference. There was no joker in the deck. Even then, you could not open with seven players still to act, and the joker makes it more likely that someone has a better hand. We'll discuss that shortly. I guess I'll just have to give you a chart so you know what to open with. Here...

PLAYERS REMAINING	MINIMUM OPENERS
7	Aces, No two pair worse than kings-up
6	Aces, No two pair worse than queens-up
5	Aces, No two pair smaller than jacks-up
4	Aces or better, (includes ANY two pair)
3	Kings or better
2	Queens or better
1	Jacks with an ace
0	Jacks

Memorize that. Those of you familiar with some of my other writing on poker will complain that this advice is different from my usual suggested strategy. That's because I wanted to present these standards in a simple form that is easy to memorize.

Furthermore, this strategy has been modified to take into consideration some things that are of particular importance to women:

1. Women can open with weaker two pair than men in earlier position, because women who open pots are raised only 87 percent as often as men. This is based on a study of 7,000 hands done in 1979 and 1980 in the $20 limit game at the Horseshoe Club in Gardena, California. The study could be blemished, because many of the same women appeared in the game session after session and some of them were known as aggressive competition. However, the results are in keeping with the information gained from the dozens of interviews with both men and women on the subject. Many

men are afraid to raise aggressive women with marginal hands. Most men shy away from bluffing women. Many men prepare to just call with relatively strong hands and fool women by betting or raising after the draw. One man told me that he sometimes likes to "stick the needle in" by using such tactics. "It's 10 times better than rape and it's legal!"

2. Women can open with weaker one pair hands in later positions, for the same reasons as discussed above. As an example, I do not allow my beginning male students to open with a pair of queens when two opponents are yet to act.

Notice that you can always open with aces. Because a pair of aces is a relatively common hand, occuring once every 21 deals, you'll make more money with aces than with any other category of hand. Also note that small two pair should not open from the early positions. The mathematics of this phenomenon are complex, but they basically center on the fact that it's a lot harder to help two pair (8.3 percent chance of improvement) than a pair of aces (as much as 37 percent chance of improvement if it's an ace-joker combination). However, women are in less danger opening with two small pair than men.

I'm instructing you to open exactly as the chart dictates without grumbling. Later, as you grow more sophisticated, you can alter your basic strategy.

* * * Calling With Kings * * *

All right, pretend you had that pair of kings in first position. You felt the urge to open, but the chart forbade such action. So you passed. The next six players also passed, and the dealer opened.

Now you've got him, right? You showed discretion by not opening, because you didn't want to risk getting raised. You patiently waited for someone else to open. You're in luck; that patience has been rewarded.

It's up to you to act. You grab your chips. The idea of raising the opener occurs to you. After all, he's in last position. Everyone else had passed, so he's likely to come barging into the pot with merely a pair of jacks, right? But the chips feel heavy in your hand, and you decide to merely call. WAIT!

What the hell do you think you're doing? Do you want to lose the grocery money? You can't call with a pair of kings—EVER!

Well, all right, here's a chart that explains what you should call with, depending on the opener's position . . .

PLAYERS TO ACT AFTER OPENER	MINIMUM CALLING HAND
7	Kings-up
6	Kings-up
5	Aces, no two pair smaller than kings-up
4	Aces, no two pair smaller than queens-up
3	Aces
2	Aces
1	Aces
0	Aces

Unless you have at least a pair of aces, you must never call an opener (with the exception of some "come hands," to be discussed later). Also, two weak pair are unplayable against an early-position opener. I have made these women's standards more strict than for men. If you do specifically what these previous two charts say, you will already be making money in the target game—the $2/$4 limit in Gardena.

Just by following those instructions, you will be avoiding the two most costly mistakes made in draw poker. One is to open with weak hands in early positions. The other is to call with jacks, queens or kings.

* * * Come Hands * * *

Often you'll have a hand which you could convert into a straight or flush by drawing one card. Some of these hands should be played, and others shouldn't.

This is a country straight . . .

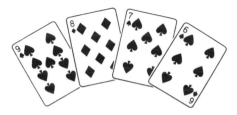

There are nine cards remaining in the deck that will turn this into a straight. These are the cards . . .

Unfortunately, there are 39 cards left in the deck that won't help (assuming you threw away a deuce). That's 3 to 1 against, and the possibility of getting this hand beaten, even if you do make it, means it's NEVER PLAYABLE!

Here are two four-flush draws . . .

The first hand should not be played. The second is worth calling an unraised pot if there are two or more opponents already involved. The rule is that a four-flush must never be played unless it includes an ace. The joker presents other unusual drawing problems. Here's a 12-way straight (12 cards can complete it) . . .

It can be played any time you would play a four-flush with an ace.

Here's a better hand, a 16-way straight . . .

If the pot isn't raised, you can always call with the hand above. There are hands with even more than 16 cards that will help them. These straight-flush draws are pretty rare and, for the sake of simplicity, they should be played just like 16-way straights.

* * * Raising * * *

If a pot is opened, what should you raise with?

Most of your opponents at this level of play will raise with aces-up or better no matter what the position of the opener. This, it turns out, is a pretty good strategy. Use it.

Since you're a woman, you can raise more liberally with two pair on occasion. This is a good image builder, but don't do it all the time. After the draw you can either play offensively or defensively depending on how timid your male adversaries are. Essentially two pair, particularly two small pair, are losers. Usually, you'll pass if there is betting. However, when there are borderline situations between passing and calling, I recommend to women that they sometimes RAISE!

If the pot is already raised, you should come in "cold" (for two bets) with three eights or better. If you have three sevens, pass.

If you open and get raised, you should fold with jacks, queens, kings and any two pair smaller than aces up. Although it's mathematically correct to throw away aces in this circumstance, it's better for your table image to call.

Stick to the formula! In Gardena there's a herd of little old male pensioners (and sadly a few female pensioners, too) who walk around mumbling, "Never bet into a one-card draw." It seems to be the only last thing on their minds.

How did you last so many years in Gardena? "I never bet into a one-card draw."

Been winning lately? "Nope. Not since last month. Can't understand it, either—I haven't been betting into one-card draws."

Although you're learning a *SIMPLE* winning formula, there is one finesse I'm going to teach you. If you hold three-of-a-kind after the draw against an opponent who's drawn one, always bet unless you're sure that player is on the come.

* * * Sandbagging * * *

Another play that involves a bit of sophistication is sandbagging (checking and then raising). It's an ideal technique which women should use occasionally to make men respect and fear them.

AS AN EVERYDAY LIFE STRATEGY, SAND-
BAGGING IS AMONG THE MOST EFFECTIVE TOOLS
WOMEN HAVE GOING FOR THEM, BECAUSE MEN
SELDOM EXPECT IT.

This is a checklist for sandbagging:

1. There are at least three players still to act behind you.
2. Your hand is kings-up or better.
3. There are no more than one jack, queen, king, ace or joker in your hand, except for a hand that includes one pair of kings or aces (and no other jack through joker).

Often choose to sandbag if all three of those conditions are true.

147

Otherwise never sandbag. All the following hands can be sand-bagged if at least five players are yet to act . . .

However, sandbagging with complete hands, such as the straight or the full house is less desirable. That's because these are strong enough to reraise if you open and a player raises. In such a case you could be playing those strong hands for three bets instead of the usual two you'll get by first checking and then raising (i.e. sandbagging).

These hands can never be sandbagged ...

The reason you don't want to sandbag with many cards in the group—*jacks, queens, kings, aces or the joker*—is that, by existing in your hand, these cards are denied to an opponent. And these are precisely the cards that will help an opponent open. Remember, your sandbag cannot succeed unless someone opens.

* * * Conclusion * * *

I've got to say this once more, because I'm sorta afraid it didn't sink in. This is *not* a sophisticated course on draw poker. From time to time in other books, seminars and columns, I've dealt with technical poker problems. For instance, I've explored in depth how to draw to hands which include both an ace and a joker. It's a good idea for you to delve into such matters once you're comfortable playing and winning at draw. But for now, you should simply employ the standard strategies while feeling your way along. Men will throw money at you if you maintain a solid, aggressive, competent image. Trust me.

Ace-joker dilemmas are beyond the scope of *this* course. You now possess a five-draw emergency kit. It permits you to set foot in the poker capital of the world, Gardena (and in other rooms throughout California and America) and win real, spendable money, even if you never heard of the place before.

The tactics you see in this course and in this book give insight into how to handle men away from the tables. And once you're comfortable with winning poker, you'll be bargaining for all the best of life's rewards and positions against men who are ill-prepared to do combat with a woman.

Not only that, if you follow this poker advice exactly, you will be the best at your table the very first time you play!

Chapter Twelve

Lowball Draw:
A Crash Course for Women

For a few minutes, I beg you to forget everything I taught you about the best and worst poker hands. Lowball draw, the way it's played in California, has the order of best-to-worst hand mostly (but not entirely) reversed.

This is the best hand you can hold ...

That's not a great hand just because it's a straight. (Remember, aces can be used as the low end of a five-high straight even in jacks-or-better high poker.) It's a great hand because it is *all* low cards and there is no pair.

Aces are always considered low, not high. And since low is best, aces are good. There's an overworked adage that goes: "Lowball isn't a game; it's a disease."

In most pubic cardrooms, they provide a separate section for low poker. That's because lowball players are very sick human beings. And because of that, management has decided that the beasts of lowball should not mingle with the gentlemen of jacks-or-better. You, however, being a woman eager to prey upon unsuspecting males, should investigate the lowball sections of the poker palaces.

As a group, lowball addicts tend to be irritable and unmannerly. They didn't start out that way. It took years and years of drawing one card to a potentially winning seven-high and missing 72.9 percent of the time to create these cranky creatures. Lowball is a series of predictable frustrations. Bad things happen to your hands MOST OF THE TIME! In standard draw poker (highball), if you draw to this hand ...

the WORST that can happen is you end up with ...

To put it simply, you can't hurt your hand. You begin with an excellent combination, and you retain that original strength while taking a *free* shot at improving. All in all, drawing can be a *comfortable* experience in jacks-or-better poker.

What about lowball? Let's say you have this hand ...

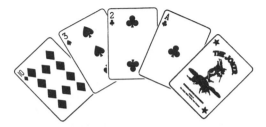

You're looking at a pat ten-high, which is good enough to win lowball pots now and then. But you're also looking at the best possible draw in the universe! In all probability you'll decide to draw a card to 3-2-A-joker, since the joker is always the lowest possible card that doesn't give you a pair. Unfortunately, 43.8 percent of the time you're fated to finish with a hand WORSE THAN WHAT YOU STARTED WITH!

That doesn't seem fair!

Lowball is a battle among ill-natured opponents who often whine and whimper, sulk and snarl. It is an angry competition spiced with animosity and aggravation. Its spirit is cold, incredibly cold, and its purpose is absolutely nonproductive.

Now I'm going to show you how to beat it!

* * * Preliminary * * *

The purpose of this course is to present a powerful, *easy* method that will instantly allow you to profit. DO NOT USE THIS TECH-NIQUE IN GAMES OF $20 LIMITS OR LARGER. These principles work best against weak-to-moderate competition. It is best to break into big-limit games in a high-hand-wins environment. The pace of the bigger limits is brisker both in physical speed and in the amount of bets and raises.

In bigger limit lowball games, you're more apt to meet a rare breed of man who will try to terrorize you with plenty of raises. That's okay, but try lowball at a smaller limit first.

This is a method to use if you're going to visit a cardroom occasionally and want to be assured of a winning expectation without putting time and concentration into mastering a really comprehensive system. This is also a very good lowball strategy to give a friend who's visiting Gardena for the first time and would like to leave with a few extra bucks.

In lowball, there are virtually no alterations women should make to the general unisex strategy. It's tougher to capitalize on being a female in lowball. There are fewer finesses available, and many men seem to call, pass or raise purely on the strength of their hands. You'll find it harder to intimidate these guys. But, as I've already mentioned, some men (especially in high-limit lowball games) will try to "bull the game" by raising women on relatively weak hands. When you spot such a man, you should call more readily. Overall, though, women can expect to be raised slightly less often than their male counterparts. It's only a small fraction of men whose strategies against women run opposite of the "play softer than against gentlemen" trend. You'll remember that in jacks-or-better-to-open draw, my statistical studies have shown that women are less frequently raised than men.

As in all my crash courses, the advice has been "smoothed out." That means that the general strategy might be slightly wrong for a few situations that arise, but will be overwhelmingly correct for most situations. All in all, this strategy has been thoroughly tested and will win.

Professional-level lowball strategies, such as my four-page "Advanced Strategy" or the section included in Doyle Brunson's *Super/System* are exceptionally powerful and I recommend them to serious students.

* * * High vs. Low Comparisons * * *

If you've ever wondered how rare certain lowball hands are compared to high hands, this segment should help you. I'm often asked questions like, "Is it harder to get a pat seven in lowball than a pat flush in high?"

The following BEFORE THE DRAW matchups show a high hand (left) that is approximately as rare as the lowball hand (right). In the first case, we see that a wheel is about as hard to get pat as queens-full or better. (Calculations are for a deck that includes a joker, which is pretty standard nowadays.)

HIGH HAND	LOW HAND

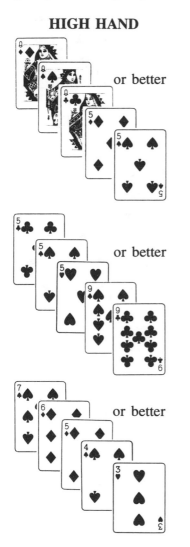

or better

or better

or better

or better

157

HIGH HAND	LOW HAND
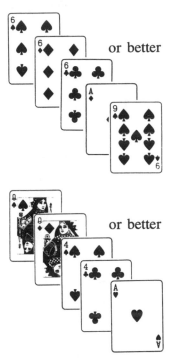 or better	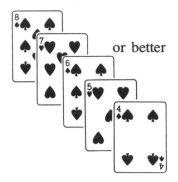 or better
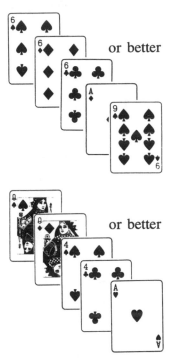 or better	 or better
Any pat straight, such as	Any pat seven, such as

Yes! Being dealt a pat seven-high straight or HIGHER is equivalent to getting a pat seven or LOWER—and that makes for good conversation.

It's also interesting that in lowball (53-card deck) a pat 8-4 (1400-1) is harder to get than a pat bicycle (1245-1). You can dazzle your grandma with that fact!

* * * Rules * * *

All that may seem pretty confusing until you understand the governing rules of lowball. Lowball draw is pretty popular in America. Most social scientists place it between Denver omelettes and pedigree kittens on a popularity scale.

In California where the game is legal and played publicly, the most common rules go like this:

1. The best hand you can get is five-four-three-two-ace of any suit;

2. Ace is the LOWEST (meaning best) card;

3. Straights and flushes don't count against you—forget they exist;

4. The limit after the draw is DOUBLE the limit before the draw;

5. Usually everyone antes and, additionally, the player to the left of the dealer puts in a BLIND bet (he MUST open the pot no matter what cards he has);

6. You can draw any number of cards from zero to five;

7. A joker is included in the deck, and it becomes whatever card would make your hand lowest. If you have eight-four-three-two-joker, the joker is an ace. With six-five-two-ace-joker, it's a three.

The object, remember, is to end up with the lowest hand. Five-four-three-two-ace beats six-five-four-three-two. King-seven-four-three-two beats six-three-two-ace-ace(pair of aces). BUT six-three-two-ace-ace beats five-four-two-two-ace (pair of deuces, aces are low).

* * * Strategy * * *

This method for beating lowball is EXTREMELY simple, but you'll find it effective and profitable.

Count the number of players remaining to your LEFT up to and including the blind. If this number is . . . four, five, six or seven, it's CONDITION SAD. Two or three it's CONDITION HAPPY; one is CONDITION ATTACK; zero is CONDITION BLIND. (Your count will be zero only if you ARE the blind.)

NOTE: Most poker books speak of player positions beginning with #1 (immediately to the dealer's left) and increasing clockwise so that, in an eight-handed game, the dealer's position is #8. As far as I know, Norman Zadeh in *Winning Poker Systems* was the first to use the excellent method of counting the players *remaining to act*. You'll remember that we used that method in the high-draw discussion.

IMPORTANT: When you're the first player (in addition to the blind) to enter a pot, this strategy dictates that you *always raise*, never just call. If your hand qualifies as a pat hand *or* a one-card draw *or* a two-card draw, you should play.

What to Raise With Before the Draw
If Everyone Before You Has Passed:

Condition	Pat Hand	1-Card Draw	2-Card Draw
Sad (no joker)	8-6-5-4-3	7-5-4-3	none
Sad (with joker)	8-7-6-5-joker	7-6-5-joker	none
Happy (no joker)	9-8-7-6-5	8-7-6-5	5-4-3
Happy (w/joker)	9-8-7-6-joker	8-7-6-joker	7-6-joker
Attack (no joker)	10-9-8-7-6	10-8-7-6	7-6-5
Attack(w/joker)	J-10-9-8-joker	10-9-8-joker	8-7-joker

Although followers of my more advanced writing may quibble with the simplicity of this formula, it wins easily against the kind of unsophisticated competition you find in public card parlors. It is particularly good for women, because men have a tacit agreement that they will play more hands than they should when the frustrations of lowball are rubbing them wrong. They tend to be hostile toward other men whose discipline never cracks. This is probably jealousy, however, they almost never say anything to women who play sensibly all the time. Females are perfectly capable of sitting in a game and playing solid basic strategy while all the men around them go through emotional tilt from time to time. Lowball is perceived as basically a game of luck. But it isn't. Any woman playing solid poker in this mostly male environment will eventually win all the chips.

Just don't let yourself get emotionally off balance and begin playing hands you shouldn't play. Then you'll be no better off than the guys surrounding you.

* * * What To Do If It's Already Raised * * *

It is customary for the first player in the pot to raise. Occasionally, an opponent just calls, and this can cause problems. Does the opponent have a weak hand or a very strong hand he or she is trying to be cute with? My smoothed-out advice is: If your opponent has called (rather than raised) the blind, never raise. If you have a playing hand, merely call. If your hand is very strong, this will confuse your opponents and afford you leverage after the draw. When there is no raise, I want you to raise *only* if you are drawing no cards and your hand is seven-high or better (better meaning a six-high, for instance).

Your crash course makes it easy to decide what to do when someone has already raised. No matter what your *condition*, re-raise with a pat seven or better or a one-card draw to a six-high or better. Otherwise, pretend that your opponent is following the chart you've just seen and call if your hand is at least as good as what he would have needed to raise.

In other words, if he raised from CONDITION SAD, then no matter what your condition is, you need a hand equal to what YOU would have raised with had you been in his position. If your hand is weaker than what his requirement should be, pass.

There is one critical exception to this calling criteria: NEVER CALL WITH A TWO-CARD DRAW unless you're the blind opener. If you're an experienced player, you've noticed that my two-card-draw-raising advice is fairly liberal. But that's if you're the *first* player to charge only!

If you've read the previous crash course, you know that I'm not going to provide advice on ALL situations, only key situations. In all other instances, my assumption is that you'll use your own best judgment and that it will be fairly average.

The last major category of advice is what to do when you're the blind.

What to Call With When You're in Condition Blind, Depending on the Condition of the Raiser:

Raiser's Condition	Pat Hand	1-Card Draw	2-Card Draw
Sad (you have no joker)	9-8-7-6-5	8-6-5-4	none
Sad (you have joker)	9-7-6-5-joker	8-7-6-joker	7-5-joker
Happy (you have no joker)	9-8-7-6-5	8-7-6-5	6-5-4
Happy (you have joker)	9-8-7-6-joker	9-7-6-joker	8-7-joker
Attack (you have no joker)	10-9-8-7-6	10-8-7-6	7-6-5
Attack (you have joker)	J-10-9-8-joker	10-9-8-joker	8-7-joker

I suppose some of you lowball sophisticates are annoyed because this strategy doesn't follow uniformly and fit nicely on bell curves. For instance, if an opponent raises in CONDITION HAPPY, how come the minimum pat calling hand for the blind is a straight nine *with or without* the joker? Doesn't the joker make a difference?

Yes, as I've pointed out in the past, the joker makes a great deal of difference! Still, here's a formula that works just the way it is! It's my recipe, so don't mess with the ingredients or I won't be responsible for the way it tastes.

Lastly, let's look at a few other essentials. After the draw, if you and one opponent have both drawn one or more cards, bet any ten or better, ALWAYS. (The previous statement applies whether you're first to act or have already been checked to. By the way, the conventional rule in California is that you MUST bet a seven or better after the draw.)

Bluff after the draw with any pair of fours or higher. NEVER enter a pot with the intention of bluffing. THERE IS NO SITUATION IN LOWBALL WHERE YOU WOULD SHOW A PROFIT BARGING INTO THE POT WITH A HAND LIKE FOUR-FOUR-FOUR-EIGHT-EIGHT. (If you can't trust the *Mad Genius*, who can you trust?) If you have a pat nine or ten with a one-card seven draw (or better), it's usually best *not* to stand pat. In fact, for the purpose of simplicity (and there are many practical exceptions), I'm instructing you to stand pat ONLY if you're against a SINGLE opponent who has already drawn at least two cards.

You should usually draw one card to this hand . . .

* * * **Final Warning** * * *

Most money is lost at lowball because players become emotionally upset. There's a great deal of short-term luck involved, and you'll need to develop a stable temperament. Without it, you're apt to find your mind short-circuited after a few bad beats. Your fingers will begin to fling chips toward the center of the table without your permission. I call this "lowball reflex."

Women are designed by nature and by temperament to be the best lowball players alive. Still, lowball is a game that eats away at your better judgment and begs you to play hands you shouldn't play, especially when you're losing. When fate is finding new friends across the table, you might find it difficult to leave the game. In fact, you could even wither away and die. So please be careful.

Chapter Thirteen

Seven-Stud:
A Crash Course for Women

This following strategy is a modified-for-women version of my previously published seven-stud course. The different forms of poker (such as jacks-or-better-to-open draw and ace-to-five lowball draw, which you've already learned about) are numerous, but seven-stud is among the most popular.

Many of the tactics that work best when used by women against men are particularly powerful in seven-stud. These include choosing seats that force macho types to act first, disarming and neutralizing dangerous men (especially one to your left) by befriending or flirting, and taking an unexpected forceful approach (heavy bets and raises), which tends to bewilder male opponents and put them at your mercy.

Seven-stud, which is played routinely at home poker games and in Las Vegas casinos, may soon be legalized in California (where only draw poker is legal now). It affords the best opportunity for women to prosper at poker.

This strategy, which is based on the one I devised primarily for male players and was first published in *Gambling Times* magazine, has been dramatically altered in certain situations to allow women to win all the money they're entitled to.

Only 11 percent of adult American males, ages 21 to 70, have ever read a poker book. Surprised?

Well, that figure isn't based on some statistical study using error-prone sampling methods; rather, it is derived from an actual rough estimate. Even fewer women have read poker books.

To most folks, poker is casual entertainment, played for reasonable stakes. The average guy or gal is too involved with everyday problems to invest hundreds of hours mastering the very technical strategy and mathematics that relate to world class poker.

What busy women need are simple poker formulas that work. Then they can use proven psychological techniques to confuse and astonish male adversaries. It's simply a matter of playing basic winning poker with a feminine flair. And you can do it. So, let's learn the basics of seven-stud.

Wouldn't it be terrific if you could stride proudly into a Las Vegas casino, sit at a $1 to $4 limit seven-stud table and destroy the game in an hour or two? If you only knew the correct strategy for small-limit seven-stud, you could vacation in Las Vegas any time you felt like it, and it wouldn't cost anything. In fact, you'd make money—modest wins of $80 to $500 on the average. And almost all of that profit would come directly from men.

Unfortunately, you don't know the formula. Yet.

Remember, this is a crash course in seven-stud. That means the advice was sort of "smoothed out" and sometimes it doesn't provide the optimum strategy for an exact situation. Even so, you'll win nicely overall. You have my promise. Besides, strategic finesse based on involved mathematical calculations are of limited value to beginning players. Although I sometimes tackle such finesses in depth at seminars, the predominantly male audience can expect them to add only 20 to 30 percent to their annual earnings.

By contrast, beyond the poker basics, just being a woman surrounded by male egos can double or triple your earnings if you act effectively. There is absolutely no question that skilled women players can earn more at poker than skilled men players.

Although the seven-stud formula given is aimed specifically at the $1 to $4 limit game, it works great for similar ranges such as $1 to $3, and the concepts can be readily adapted to larger limits, like $5 and $10. Also these principles work well for home poker games. Let these be the groundwork for higher-limit poker.

You and I owe a really massive amount of thanks to a guy named Rick Grieder. Although Rick has quietly remained out of the poker spotlight, most big-name players respect him as a tremendous talent.

But hardly anyone knows this: For two years, Rick averaged five hours a day *away* from the poker tables working on seven-stud.

Grieder is a world class authority on seven-stud. That is meant as a tribute to someone who never got his fair share of recognition.

After I formulated my guidelines for small-limit seven-stud, Rick agreed to go over these point-by-point, making some additions and modifications—based on the practical experience of his students who play regularly in Las Vegas. Although our strategy makes many compromises for the sake of simplicity and is definitely not intended without common-sense modification for a high-stakes game against accomplished opponents, we both sincerely believe that if you use this method, you must win.

Here's a description of the specific game this formula is suited to, although the advice is also applicable to winning at other seven-stud games.

The limit is $1 to $4, which means a player has an option of betting or raising in amounts of $1, $2, $3 or $4.

Here's how seven-stud is played: Whether at home or in casinos, the players are each dealt three cards, two down, one up. Like this ...

The cards face down are secret and only you may look at them. The one face up is exposed to you and all your opponents, so they can use it to make evaluations about the strength of your hand. A complete seven-stud hand consists of seven cards, three of them face down and four face up. Like this . . .

The jack of spades, king of hearts, deuce of diamonds and ten of clubs are seen by everyone. Let's suppose these are your face-down cards . . .

Only you see them, and you must choose your best combination of five cards (remember, five cards make up a typical poker hand) from among all seven (three down, four up).

In the previous example, what is the strength of your hand? It's not a pair of jacks, even though you do have two jacks present. In fact, you have a much better hand than jacks—an ace-high straight. These are the five cards, selected from all seven that provide you with that straight . . .

If you don't like the jack of diamonds, you can substitute the jack of spades.

In many Vegas cardrooms, after the first three cards are dealt the lowest exposed card (each player has one) is "forced" to make an initial token wager of half a dollar (called "bringing it in"). This may come in addition to a dime ante. The lowest card "brings it in" because that is thought to stimulate action. (In many home games and in some casinos, no such rule applies. The high card showing can either bet or check as he or she chooses.) The action then continues clockwise until all players have acted in the traditional call-raise-pass method that governs poker.

There are two frequent variations. One is no ante. The other, high card brings it in for half a dollar. If either of these rules applies, you should play somewhat less liberally.

There are betting rounds after the third, fourth, fifth, sixth and seventh cards. The last card is then dealt face down. If you raise on any given round, that raise must at least equal the amount of the bet. In other words, if a guy bets $3, you must put in $6 ($3 to call and $3 to raise) if you want to make it more expensive.

I'll be using the term "street" here. That's simply the conventional way of describing the number of cards that have been dealt to each contestant so far. The first betting round is on third street, the last on seventh street.

Ready?

Many times a casino will have more than one $1 to $4 limit game. You might watch these games for a few minutes. The ideal choice for this strategy is the one with the most players per pot with a minimum amount of raises. That's because, in any kind of poker, you'll make the most money against timid opponents who call with weak hands but don't get maximum value out of their strong hands. Try to pick a table with no other women who could compete for attention and deny you the queen-of-your-table title.

Don't worry about the competition being too tough. You'll almost never find sophisticated players at this level. They're just there to have fun and give away a little money. Might as well take it, don't you think?

Go ahead and sit down.

In terms of profit, whether you play your first three cards or not is the most critical decision you'll need to make.

These are the important considerations:

1. The strength of your hand.

2. How many players are yet to act behind you. (The more there are, the more vulnerable your hand is.)

3. The exposed (up cards) of your opponents.

Of course, there are other factors as well, such as how much it will cost to call and how many other players are active. But our formula ignores these aspects. For instance, if you think you have the best pair, raise no matter what. If you have a large three-flush, call for up to $2.

Starting requirements filter down to this: If you have better than three jacks, an ace-high three-flush or three parts of a straight-flush, just call and try to keep players in. If you have trips smaller than jacks or the probable best pair, raise and chase players out.

* * * Examples * * *

With these starting hands, you should raise and chase players out . . .

(Of course, you might not even play the pair of queens or the pair of tens. If you do, raise.)

With these starting hands, you should just call and keep players in . . .

Got it? If you do that and the rest of your game is just average, you're already doing well enough to make money against weak competition!

If you hold this set of trips or higher . . .

you should simply call whatever the bet is on third street, even if it's only 50 cents. Wait until fourth street, then bet $4 every chance you get, unless you feel someone has a better hand. Don't expect to start with a hand this good very often. The odds against it are 1,380 to 1.

With a lesser three-of-a-kind, raise $2 if the bet is only 50 cents. If someone has already made it more than 50 cents, raise $4.

Play a pair of aces and kings the same way.

Now we come to the tricky stuff—pairs less than kings. If a king in an early position bets, say, $2 and you have Q-Q-2, THROW IT AWAY!

DON'T EVER CALL WITH A PAIR OF QUEENS OR LESS IF A PLAYER SHOWS STRENGTH BY BETTING WITH A HIGHER CARD. However, here's an important area where a correct woman's strategy differs from a correct man's strategy. You should frequently choose to *raise* with a pair of queens or less when a male opponent has bet with a higher card showing!

Actual casino experiments have proven that men who habitually bet aggressively throughout an entire seven-stud hand, are inclined to check on all subsequent betting rounds when a woman makes an early raise on third street. That's because macho men DON'T LIKE TO BE THE AGGRESSORS WHEN THEY ARE CONFUSED BY A WOMAN. That principle holds up in poker, in life beyond poker, and possibly in life beyond life. In other words, it is a very powerful concept.

> MEN LIKE TO BE AGGRESSIVE TO CONFUSE AND
> DOMINATE WOMEN. THEY TEND NOT TO BE
> AGGRESSIVE WHEN THEY ARE, THEMSELVES,
> CONFUSED.

So raise with those vulnerable pairs against macho men showing bigger cards. Chances are they'll back off and become timid. This means, it will be your choice later in the hand whether to play offensively. It will be your choice, because the guy will quit betting. He'll give up and yield control of the wagering to you. That's a huge advantage. Try it. This strategy specifically does *not* usually work when a male uses it against another male.

The bottom line is that women can safely raise on third street (the first three cards) with small pairs against men, whereas men holding the same cards could not even profitably play!

You should keep in mind that if your opponent does have a pair on his first three cards, two out of three times it will be of the exposed denomination. Therefore, usually ASSUME A BETTOR HAS A PAIR OF HIS DOOR CARD (the exposed card). However, common sense suggests that if an opponent bets with a three showing, he's unlikely to have merely a pair of threes.

SELDOM PLAY PAIRS SMALLER THAN TENS AGAINST MORE THAN ONE OPPONENT. If you do play such a pair against two or more males, raise, don't just call. With any pair on third street, either raise or throw your hand away if no one else has bet already.

Rick defines the key to winning as "isolating your pair head-up against an opponent with a lesser pair." That's true of all forms of seven-stud. When you have a pair, try to raise players out— you don't want three-way action!

Here are four other typical hands you might consider starting with . . .

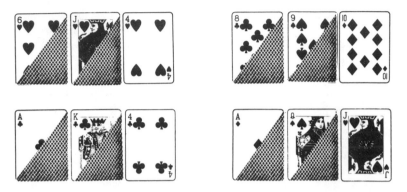

These are "come" hands, which means they can potentially become a straight or a flush. If it's only 50 cents and no one behind you is apt to raise, call with any of these. Otherwise ONLY play the three clubs. Even then, don't come in if it costs more than $2.50 (the original 50 cents plus a $2 raise).

Although the 8-9-10 may look tempting, and most large limit players call small bets to see a fourth card, these hands are very big losers in small-limit games where a large number of players compete for the pot and the average winning hand is abnormally strong.

Simply stated: On your first three cards, NEVER CALL FOR MORE THAN HALF A DOLLAR WITH ANY COME HAND EXCEPT A STRAIGHT FLUSH OR A FLUSH THAT IN-CLUDES AN ACE. This is especially true for women. Female poker players get their power over men by playing strong and mar-ginal hands aggressively. Come hands (where you have nothing yet but could connect with a straight, a flush or a straight flush) are psychologically weak weapons. They seldom allow raising and should only be played selectively.

In general, when you have one pair and it looks like the best hand, you must try to get head-up against an opponent. This is mandatory! Never (NEVER!) slow play ANY pair in small-limit seven-stud. (In larger limit games you should slow play *only* to confuse male opponents and gain a later advantage.)

174

If you have any question about whether yours figures to be the best pair, either raise or throw it away. Pay attention to the other players' door cards. Remember, it's not just the strength of your hand that's important. It's your hand in relation to your opponents' hands. Not only do the exposed cards give you an idea of what other players are betting, they often dictate whether or not you should play.

For example, seldom invest money on a pair of queens if someone has a queen for a door card. Don't ever play ANY three-card flush if two or more of your suit are showing. Is that simple enough? Well, that was the tough part. After third street, the rest is easy. Here are some important tips . . .

If an opponent has put in any action above the token 50-cent opening bet, he's often going "to the river" (to seventh street). Once a player has committed himself on third street, it's usually going to take more than a maximum $4 bet limit to scare him out. Maybe that sounds like bad poker, but usually you *also* will be going to the river once you put anything more than 50 cents into the pot on third street. That's why the play-or-not-play decision is so vitally important.

Here are two late-in-the-hand situations where you *should* throw your hand away:

1. A player bets on fourth street or fifth street after pairing his door card. (Fold one pair or two pair; the chances that the player has three of a kind are heavy.)

2. A player who's been just calling catches a third suited card on fifth street and bets. (Fold any pair, including aces, and any potential straight or small flush.)

DON'T PAY FOR A FIFTH CARD UNLESS YOU'RE PREPARED TO TAKE A SEVENTH CARD! In other words, it will require a rare event for you to throw away your hand on sixth or seventh street.

Male players should play small-limit seven-stud games in a fairly straightforward manner. That is, they shouldn't try to be tricky and sandbag. The opponents are too unsophisticated to understand what a check is supposed to mean, and therefore, won't bet marginal hands if a man tries to sandbag. Women, however, can sandbag frequently even against unsophisticated seven-stud players. That's because macho men, being macho men, like to bet into women who check.

However, you should not sandbag against a man whom you've been friendly with or have flirted with. They're apt to check out of kindness and you'll lose your betting opportunity. Against them, you should *bet* strong hands, never sandbag.

Your style of play should be straightforward. That is, don't try to be tricky. Your opponents, at this level of play, will call anyway. Sandbagging (checking and then raising) is out!

Men can seldom bluff profitably in these low-limit stud games, but women can on occasion. Always bluff using crisp, dynamic, confident movements which guys don't expect from gals. It works.

You can occasionally try to steal the ante and the "bring in" bet if you're LAST TO ACT. Raise $1. If you get reraised, give it up. If you get called, give it up—that is, don't bet on fourth street and, if you get bet into, pass.

Seven-stud is an ideal battle ground for male vs. female ego wars. Here, the male egos are outgunned, but overconfident. A lot of luck is involved in stud and it sometimes takes time for skill to prove profitable. The fluctuations of fortune in seven-stud are frustrating to a man who wants to prove his superiority in an hour. Women must only use psychology and have patience to prosper.

Chapter Fourteen

Hold 'Em:
A Crash Course for Women

Again, here is another of my previously published courses which has been restructured for women. Most of the changes allow you to play more aggressively and win bigger than men could using a similar strategy.

Let's do something different. You get to ask questions and I get to answer. Actually, I get to both ask and answer, but you'll live the illusion of having asked. Okay?

First, let me tell you that hold 'em is another popular kind of poker. In some ways, it is related to seven-stud but, in fact, it is not really a form of seven-stud because its style and strategy are very different.

Every year in May there's a poker tournament held at Binion's Horseshoe in downtown Las Vegas. It's the richest and most prestigious event in all of poker. For the past three years, there's been more than a million dollars ($1,000,000.00) in prize money, made up of the $10,000-per player entry fees.

Every year more than 100 of the best pros in the world have battled to be crowned the king of poker for the year. But alas, never has a queen of poker emerged from this tournament. Maybe that's because fewer than 2 percent of participants have been female.

Anyway, the poker game that determines the world champion is hold 'em, so you'd better learn how to play. Maybe one year soon you'll want to give it a shot, and perhaps be the first champion of poker who is also a woman. A woman as the reigning monarch of poker! It could happen someday; and it should.

Why is hold 'em the game that determines the world champion of poker every year at Binion's?

See, there came the first question, and you weren't even expecting it. The reason it's the world championship game is because an all-male herd of Texans and Texas sympathizers got together about 15 years ago and decided to hold the first world poker championship. Texans, and most southerners, prefer hold 'em above all other forms of poker. The championship was played (Johnny Moss won) and a precedent was established. Hold 'em was forced upon the rest of us. Fans of draw poker and seven-stud had figured that one of those two forms was the main game. But these Texans suddenly pushed hold 'em forever into the spotlight. It was definitely a *coup d'etat.*

You sound almost bitter. Are you?

Naw. Not anymore. But you should be suspect of hold 'em being the big game. Females in the south, where it's most popular, are seldom invited to participate.

Will you teach me, a mere woman, the rules of hold 'em?

Yes, provided you don't say where you got this information. First of all, you get dealt a hand; for instance . . .

That's not a hand; that's just two cards! Is this a mistake?

I'm afraid not. Those two cards are your entire private hand until a winner is decided.

What do you mean my private hand? Is there such a thing as a public hand?

Exactly. There will be five cards turned face up by the dealer, and these will belong equally to every player. Remember that, in one trivial sense, hold 'em is a variation of seven-stud. You choose your best five-card hand among seven cards: the two secret cards that comprise your private hand and the five public cards face up on the table.

For example, suppose you started with the hand previously illustrated (a pair of fours). There is an initial round of betting. Typically about six of the ten players will throw their hands away. (Yes, *ten* is a common number of participants in hold 'em. You can play with any number from 2 to 22.) Now three cards are turned face up by the dealer. This is called the flop. Let's say this is the flop . . .

Now you already have two pair, kings over fours. (But you really don't have a powerful hand because *everybody* has *at least* a pair of kings! Think about it.) There's another round of betting. Next the dealer turns a fourth card face up on the table. It's a six of spades. More betting. Then the fifth and final card, a king of diamonds. In the end, the board (the five cards face up common to every player) looks like this . . .

179

You have a full house—three kings and two fours—but it could easily be beaten by any player holding a king (four kings), an eight (kings full over eights), a six (kings full over sixes) or a pair larger than your fours (a better kings full). Now comes a last round of betting and the winner is determined.

In general, the conventional rules of poker apply: act in turn, action moves clockwise, etc. You might want to consult some other source for special rules, but basically you know enough to play. In some games everyone antes. Typically there's no ante, but one or more players to the dealer's left are required to make blind opening bets. In any case, the advice provided here is so universal that it will help you with almost any hold 'em structure.

All right. I sorta understand how to play. What's a great hand to start with?

Most beginners assume that the hand in the first example, four-four, is good. In fact, it's one of the most costly hands in limit hold 'em. (In no-limit games, it frequently has a better potential. But today, we're talking about limit hold 'em.) You should seldom, if ever, play a pair smaller than sevens.

As you would expect, your best hand is ace-ace, followed by king-king. You might think that this sequence of strength continues: queen-queen, jack-jack, ten-ten, nine-nine, eight-eight, right on down to deuce-deuce.

Don't think like that! In hold 'em ace-king is a much, much more powerful hand than six-six. In fact, ace-king is more profitable than ten-ten or jack-jack. And in some eight-to-ten-handed games, it's better than queen-queen! (In most cases I favor the queen-queen, contrary to the advice of many other authorities.)

That ace-king is in the same league with queen-queen is hard to grasp, so let's talk about it. Suppose you hold . . .

Now the flop (remember, these three cards are turned face up by the dealer and belong to everybody) is . . .

Novices don't really grasp the danger here. Generally, there are two or more opponents still competing. There's a better than average chance that they're playing high cards (which is the key to hold 'em). Sure, you started with a pair of queens, and it's very hard to get a starting hand that good. If you really want to know, you'll only get a starting pair that strong once in 74 hands. Okay, so you might be inclined to feel pretty smug. You might think you've got your male opponents in a sad way. But look at that flop. If any one of those opponents holds a single ace or a single king, you no longer have the best hand!

It's very likely you're beat at this point. And don't be surprised if you're beat in two places! When you hold a pair of queens, you should hope for a flop like . . .

The concept is that when you hold a pair, you want to either make three of a kind or see all lower cards flop. The smaller your pair, the more difficult this latter trick becomes.

Here comes a specific answer to your question. These are the best hands to start with in hold 'em . . .

Those are the best five hands you'll ever see. Remember: aces, kings, queens, ace-king suited, ace-king unsuited. Unfortunately, you'll only get one of these hands every 39 deals on average.

You'd always stay to see the flop with any of those five best hands, wouldn't you?

As a practical matter, in a limit game you will seldom throw away any of the big five hands without seeing the flop. Be warned, however, that if the raising gets very hot, there is only one hand that you would never throw away, no matter what. That's a pair of aces.

Which hands would I raise with?

As in all forms of poker, use your best judgement about whether or not to raise. Beginners believe they should always raise with king-king or queen-queen. This isn't true. It's often better just to see the flop cheaply. There's a good chance you won't like it, and then you can withdraw from the competition inexpensively. In hold 'em, you usually won't know until after the flop whether you *really* have a good hand or bad hand! However, women should be much more willing to raise with a pair of jacks or tens before the flop than should men. Just as in seven-stud, this causes many normally aggressive men to surrender their lead and check to you for an entire hand. Because you have raised early, many men will become instinctively confused by this perceived role reversal (i.e., aggression on your part) and allow you to keep the initiative.

Okay, but I can't sit around humming happily until I get one of those five super hands or some other big pair. I don't have that much patience.

Believe me, I understand. That's why there are a lot more hands you can play under the right conditions. Let's add ...

You will almost always see the flop with these hands, too. But if someone raises the first bettor (often a blind bettor) and then there's a reraise, you should consider who's doing the raising. Do not call routinely. Adding this group to our list of playable hands, we can now play one out of 25 deals (excluding pairs smaller than kings which you, as a woman, can play selectively).

Big deal. I want ACTION. Can't you find me some more hands to play?

Sure. Add these to your list ...

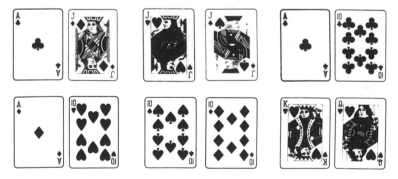

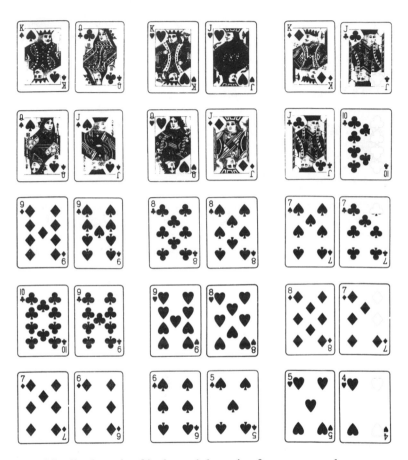

Specifically the pair of jacks and the pair of tens are much stronger hands for women (as I've already pointed out) than they are for men. Therefore, you should occasionally raise with them if you have a shot at winning and can thereby bring a man from a dominant to a passive role. The same is true to a lesser extent for slightly smaller pairs.

Those hands aren't pictured in the exact order of their strength. Rather they are shown in a sequence that is fairly easy to remember. All of these hands should be played with caution, and you should never enter a pot cold if it's been raised and re-raised before the action gets to you. Also, you will seldom play these hands from an early position.

Are there any other hands I can start with?

Not unless you're pretty sure you can see the flop cheaply (i.e., without having to call a raise). In very late positions, you can sometimes play hands like . . .

The pair of sixes is the most costly for beginners. If you decide never to play any hands like that, you won't be sacrificing much. What's important is to understand the hands that are the biggest long-range losers. Look at these . . .

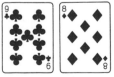

Those hands are very tempting for novices. But they're all long-range losers.

Chapter Fifteen

Concepts and Applications

We will now review some of the winning concepts you've learned and add some new thoughts. Poker is not merely a specific game, but a miniature proving ground for life's challenges. Many of the best poker principles are applicable every day, all over the place.

You can beat male adversaries at the poker table; and you can also beat them beyond the table. Let's talk about it.

What's the first thing you've got to ask yourself when involved in any real-life situation with a man? You should ask this question: *Is poker being played?* Many of the proven tactics discussed on the previous pages can only be effective if you're involved in a "game of poker." As you now know, poker doesn't have to be a formal game of cards. It can be anything involving analogous elements, even though they may be hard to find and define.

It might be difficult for you at first to decide if poker's being played. But keep asking mentally, wherever you are, and soon the answer will be clear and instantaneous. You'll know for sure whether or not you're confronted with a poker opportunity. When you can do that, you'll own a bigger share of success than you ever dared dream.

Not all of life's involvements are like poker. Many call for co-operation instead of competition. Sometimes, there are situations in which there can be more than one main winner. Sometimes all participants can come out ahead. Sometimes, there is no clearly defined pot and you must go about your business making strides forward almost by accident. These non-poker-like events are commonplace, and it's important that you be able to tell when the game being played is similar to poker and when it isn't. When it is, you can apply the same powerful strategies that work so well for you at the card table. Especially against men.

Here are four elements that help you to determine whether the game is poker:

1. *Is there an ante, a blind bet or something worth fighting over?* In poker, it's usual for players to invest a small token wager before seeing their cards.

    The ante is the incentive for the following struggle to win the pot. Sometimes a different method is used, called blind opening. In that case, one or more players are required to make an opening wager without looking at their cards—and the opponents can then call, pass or raise. Those blind bets, like the antes, are an incentive for you to get involved in the pot.

    In order for poker to be played, there must be that original incentive. Both you and your opponent (or several opponents) must have something worth competing for. Perhaps it's recognition from the boss, luring an investor to your side, making your husband/boyfriend see things your way or winning a head-of-department promotion away from a male challenger at your college. Poker can only be played properly if there's something that you and your opponents want, but only one of you can have. It always starts with a pot, which means there must be something akin to an ante, and that pot may or may not grow bigger.

2. *You must have a hand.* You can't play poker without cards or something that substitutes for cards. Whenever you face a new situation, you must ask yourself if you have the elements that make up a hand. Without these, you cannot play the game. In truth, you *always* have some kind of a hand

in every poker-like situation. It will sometimes be very powerful, but usually it won't be. It's up to you to decide whether or not to play.

For instance, you may be after a refund at the drugstore, but you've lost your receipt. You must then decide whether a confrontation with the manager is worth the effort. In other words, when you look at the size of the pot (getting your refund) relative to what you have to invest (aggravation, time and possibly embarrassment), you must decide whether your hand (you have no receipt, but you did make the purchase) is strong enough to play. Maybe you feel you can bluff your way through. In any event, in order to make such decisions, you must visualize that you're holding some sort of a poker hand.

3. *Your hand must be secret.* If everything about your real-life "poker hand" were known to the opposition, then you couldn't make reasonable bets, bluffs or raises. You could still use strategy, but the game would not be poker.

4. *The main pot must be destined for one individual.* For instance, if you're gambling on getting a job, trying to win an argument or attempting to make a child behave, there is a single pot at stake that will either be awarded to you or your opponent. Sure, you may conjure up some compromises along the way, just as you might agree to split a pot rather than play out a hand at a real poker table. But the original understanding is that there's basically one pot (although in real life it can be complex and made up of many things, some abstract) and that it will be awarded to a single winner. Poker requires this.

So, the four things you should ask to decide if you're playing poker are:

1. Is there an ante in the pot worth pursuing?

2. Do I have a hand?

3. Is my hand a secret?

4. Can only one person win the pot?

If all those answers are *yes*, it's time to play poker.

* * *

Just like in formal poker, you should only play hands which promise a long-range profit. You should not play every hand. In fact, you should not play most hands.

* * *

Always ask yourself if there are opening requirements. Remember how it was in jacks-or-better-to-open? You couldn't make that first bet unless you held some minimum standard. The same may be true in your business dealings. Maybe you need special credentials for a promotion. Make sure you understand the game, and if openers are required, be certain you have them before investing your time and energy.

* * *

When you're having a poker-like real-life encounter with male adversaries, speak crisply and decisively (just as you bet crisply at the table). Understand what a bet or a raise really is. It need not involve money or even direct promises. All it has to do is INCREASE THE INTENSITY OF THE STRUGGLE. That's exactly what a bet or raise does.

When you're in a heated argument, for instance, you automatically have a tendency to raise by shouting louder. You could even raise by sulking, since it adds to the intensity. But these kinds of raises are usually unprofitable. It's like being emotionally upset at the poker table and throwing away extra money on a losing hand.

Besides taking crisp and decisive actions against male opponents, try to convey calmness and confidence when you bet or raise.

* * *

Always try to think ahead. What are the possible consequences of your bet or your raise? Usually there will be several, so you should be prepared for more than one response from your opponents. After you've analyzed your next move, you need to have a back-up plan if things don't go in the most likely direction. Players who think ahead can get away with more daring strategies than players who don't. That's especially true for women, since men tend to be more lenient with their unexpected behavior.

* * *

When you're involved in a poker-like experience, always identify which players are apt to have their say *before* you and which are apt to speak or maneuver *after* you. Just as in poker, there is a great advantage in acting last. Always try to make macho men commit themselves first. You've already learned that in poker it is highly profitable to act after your most knowledgeable and aggressive opponents.

Also, try to act after the non-aggressive players who probably don't belong in the pot. Remember, these are the ones who play almost every pot weakly, and pose no real threat. You really want them involved, so you can manipulate them if need be and also you can look good by comparison. If you act before they do and raise the intensity, you'll chase them out of the pot. Weak players should usually be welcome in your pots, not discouraged from playing. You will gain much by acting after these guys, and can often them use as springboards to solidify your strategies. For instance, if you're contending for a job, you'll profit by letting these weaker players speak first.

Players in real-life who never raise the level of intensity (mild-mannered reporters from the *Daily Planet*), and who play their cards in a straightforward, sensible manner can be allowed to safely act after you.

* * *

No matter what, if almost all of your opponents are male, NEVER LET ANOTHER WOMAN ACT AFTER YOU (assuming you have an alternative). Remember to be queen of your table—even when there is no table!

* * *

In life, if you're bluffing, never threaten a male opponent. Worst thing you could do. Simply, IMPLY THAT YOU HAVE A GOOD HAND BY BETTING CONFIDENTLY.

* * *

Keep in mind that it doesn't matter how good your hand is in absolute terms, only how good it is for a given situation. You may be bidding on a contract using the best terms you've ever offered. But if someone is clearly making a better offer, back off and lay down that "big hand" without a fight. Soon, you might commit your energy to a much more profitable situation, even though with a weaker hand. That next hand will be STRONG FOR THE SITUATION. And it will win!

* * *

As a woman, you can try strategies that would be inappropriate for men. If all else fails, you can be more aggressive and less tactful than men. Culturally, men must not intrude too far into alien territory because they fear physical or verbal abuse. Not so with women. You can step right in where you "don't belong" and attempt tactics guys never get away with. You're just a woman who "doesn't know better." You'll never get punched out; and you'll probably never get yelled at.

* * *

Practice lying. David Hayano, professor of anthropology at Cal State Northridge, wrote a great research paper on the correlation between bluffing at poker and lying in everyday life. I honestly think lying is a weak skill with most women. They tend to only lie defensively (i.e., in order to cover up), whereas—every businessman knows—aggressive lying (making things up to gain ground) is one of the best tactics in the universe. (I don't use it, by the way.)

Give exemptions to your friends and lovers, your kids and your neighbors. Practice on those you perceive as your opponents. You'll soon be able to bluff or to lie instantly when it's appropriate.

* * *

Don't forget, you don't need to get involved in *this* pot. YOU'LL ALWAYS HAVE ANOTHER HAND TO PLAY, SO BE SELECTIVE.

* * *

When you raise by increasing the tension, do so early and then frequently expect your male adversaries to be unsure and to stop betting for the rest of the hand.

* * *

One of the worst things you can do is just call a man every time he raises the tension. Often you should either withdraw from competition or raise by increasing the level yourself.

* * *

Flirt with or befriend men who will act *after* you. Declare war on those who must act *first*.

* * *

Use poker-like finesses. If you hold a big hand, try for a sandbag situation. Suppose you and a male colleague have been secretly researching a project, knowing that your boss will want to have your input. You both also know that it's in your vital interest to impress him more than the other.

You're both called into his office together for three way consultation. Those are the makings of a poker hand, right?

The boss asks you, "Do you know what the cost is going to be for the Main Street expansion?"

Clearly the boss has determined that it's your turn to act. You would have rather had your colleague go first, since that would have given you a positional advantage.

So you check to him. How? You say, "I really don't know *exactly*."

The boss shrugs, a little unhappy but not surprised by your lack of knowledge. He turns to the other player (the *man*). "Frank, do you have any idea?"

"It's a tough one to estimate," Frank booms, "but I'd say anywhere from two hundred thousand to a quarter million."

He's acted and now it's your turn. "Oh, it's going to cost considerably more than that," you barge in. "In fact, the low estimate is $322,000 and it could range to $425,000 depending on whether we can secure those labor contracts." You reach into your attache case. "Here's a breakdown of 37 major factors, with the high and low estimate for each. Some are fixed costs, so the high and low columns are the same."

Frank is gaping. Not a happy man.

The boss says, "I thought you didn't know the cost exactly." He's smiling at you.

"Not *exactly*," you explain. "As you can see, there's a large gap between . . . "

Check and raise! See how nice that sandbag worked?

Had you gone ahead and spoken first, Frank would have calmly listened and then added in his most manly tone, "I really expect that it will be on the lower side. That's a pretty big gap between high and low. Let me try to refine her figures over the weekend, so you'll have a better outlook."

He would have won the pot! But you made him act first and then you won it with a perfect sandbag.

* * *

Practice the tactics you've learned on these pages. Keep looking for poker situations in everyday life. The first day you may only find one or two. But after a month of effort, you'll find poker being played almost everywhere you look.

That's good news, because poker's your game, isn't it?

GLOSSARY

A Selection of Poker Terms

ACE: The highest ranking card in poker.

ACE-TO-FIVE LOWBALL: A form of draw poker in which the low hands win, five-four-three-deuce-ace construed as the best hand. (Game covered in Chapter 12.)

ALL IN: When a player has wagered all the money available to him or her.

AMARILLO SLIM: Won the Binion World Series of Poker in 1972.

ANTE: An investment, usually one chip, placed in the pot by each player before the cards are dealt. The combined antes provide the incentive for poker combat.

BOBBY BALDWIN: Won the Binion World Series of Poker in 1978.

BICYCLE: The lowest and, therefore, best hand in ace-to-five lowball: five-four-three-deuce-ace.

BLIND: A required opening bet made by a player (usually the first player to the left of the dealer). It's intended to stimulate action.

BLUFF: To bet an inferior hand in the hope that an opponent will fold a hand that would have won.

BOARD: The five communal cards turned face up in the center of the table in hold 'em. ("There were two pair showing on the board.") Also the exposed cards of any seven-stud hand. ("I'm studying his board.")

BRING IT IN: Make the first wager. Usually this is a mandatory token bet—as in seven-stud when either the high card showing or the low card showing must bet to start the action.

DOYLE BRUNSON: Won the Binion World Series of Poker back to back in 1976 and 1977.

BET: To make a wager.

BUTTON: A marker sometimes used to locate the position of the player who *would be* dealer if a professional one weren't used.

BUY-IN: The amount of money required to enter a poker game.

CALL: To put an amount of money or chips into the pot equal to the bet. Calling keeps a player eligible to win a pot.

CHECK: To temporarily decline to bet while reserving the option to call, pass or raise if an opponent bets.

CHECK-RAISE: Sandbag.

COME HAND: A hand which has no real value yet, but is played on speculation, usually with the hope of making a straight or a flush.

COUNTRY STRAIGHT: Four cards whose ranks are in sequence and allow a chance at making a straight by catching one more appropriate card (lower or higher). Example: 7-6-5-4.

CUT: After the dealer has shuffled, he or she customarily offers the deck to a player on the right. That player then divides the deck into two parts and the dealer reverses the order of those parts before distributing the poker hands. In public casinos, professional dealers (who do not participate in the poker competition) usually cut their own cards after shuffling.

DECK: A collection of 52 playing cards made up of four suits, each having 13 cards ranking (high to low): ace, king, queen, jack, ten, nine, eight, seven, six, five, four, three, deuce (or two).

DEUCE: The lowest ranking card in poker. Also called a two.

DRAW: To discard and then request replacement cards from the dealer in an effort to improve a hand. Also, five-card draw poker. (Game covered in Chapter 11.)

FLOP: After the first round of betting in hold 'em, three cards are turned face up on the table. These are called the flop.

FLUSH: A poker hand with all five cards having the same suit. Ranks above a straight and below a full house.

FOLD: To pass and surrender all rights to the pending pot.

FOUR FLUSH: Four cards of the same suit, requiring one more of that suit to make a flush.

FOUR OF A KIND: A poker hand in which four of the five cards have the same rank, such as 9-9-9-9-2. Beats a full house and loses to a straight flush.

HAL FOWLER: Won the Binion World Series of Poker in 1979.

FULL HOUSE: A five-card poker hand containing both three-of-a-kind and a pair, such as:

Beats a flush and loses to a four-of-a-kind.

HAND: Five cards dealt to a poker player upon which he or she will compete for a pot. Or, any number of cards controlled by a player during a hand in poker. Or, the first two private cards dealt to a player in hold 'em. Also, one round of poker from the shuffle until a winner is determined.

HEADS UP: Two people playing poker.

HOLD 'EM: The form of poker used to determine the world champion every year during the World Series of Poker at Binion's

Horseshoe in Las Vegas. In a sense, it's a form of seven-stud. (Game covered in Chapter 14.)

IGNORANT END: In hold 'em, the low end of a straight.

INSIDE STRAIGHT: Four cards which could make a straight if one exact rank is drawn "inside." Example:

You'd need a seven.

JACKS-OR-BETTER: A form of draw poker in which a player must have at least a pair of jacks to make the first wager.

JOKER: A standard wild card. Often it is limited in scope and can only be used as an ace or to complete a straight, a flush or a straight flush.

JACK KELLER: Won the Binion World Series of Poker in 1984.

LOOSE: Liberal play.

LOWBALL: Various forms of low-hand-wins poker. Ace-to-five is the most common.

TOM McEVOY: Won the Binion World Series of Poker in 1983.

JOHNNY MOSS: Won the Binion World Series of Poker in 1971 and 1974.

NO PAIR: A hand without a pair. In conventional poker, the worst category of hand.

ON THE COME: Playing a come hand.

ON TILT: Emotionally upset and playing poorly.

OPEN-END STRAIGHT: Country straight.

OPENER: The player who made the first bet.

OPENERS: The hand held by the opener when he or she made the first bet. To show openers in jacks-or-better means to prove you had the minimum hand required to open (a pair of jacks).

PAIR: Two cards of the same rank, such as 8-8 or king-king. The second lowest category of poker hand, beats no pair, loses to two pair.

PASS: To fold. Loosely, to check.

PAT: Needing no cards on the draw.

PUGGY PEARSON: Won the Binion World Series of Poker in 1973.

POSITION: The legal order in which a player will act on his hand relative to the first player and to the dealer. (Late-acting positions are usually more profitable.)

POT: The collective chips and money wagered by poker players which will be awarded to the winner of the hand.

RAISE: In response to a bet, to put more than enough chips or money required to call.

RAP: To thump or tap the table, usually with a fist. It means either that the player wants to draw no cards or that he's checking to an opponent.

RIVER: The final card in seven-stud or hold 'em is the river card. If that card makes your hand, you've "caught down the river."

SAILOR ROBERTS: Won the Binion World Series of Poker in 1975.

ROYAL FLUSH: The highest ranking category of poker hand. Actually it's an ace-high straight flush.

SANDBAG: To first check with a strong poker hand, then raise an opponent who subsequently bets.

SEVEN-STUD: A form of poker in which players select their best five-card hands from among seven cards. (Game covered in Chapter 13.)

SLOW PLAY: To underplay a hand deceptively—just calling when a raise seems desirable or checking when a bet is appropriate. The object is to trick an opponent into thinking your hand is weak.

SOFT PLAY: To play less aggressively than desirable against an opponent, usually out of friendship or kindness. This tactic is bad for you and bad for poker.

SPLIT: To agree to divide a pot between the participants without playing the hand to conclusion. Often the rules of a particular poker game forbid splitting pots this way. Sometimes there's a tie for best poker hand and the pot is split among the co-winners. Also, in jacks-or better draw poker, splitting openers means to discard one or more of the cards that made up legal openers with the hope of making a much better hand.

STARTING HAND: Your first two cards in hold 'em, which are kept secret from your opponents. Your first three cards in seven-stud, two face down and one face up.

STEAMING: On tilt.

STRAIGHT: A poker hand with five cards ranking in sequence, such as 8-7-6-5-4. Beats three of a kind and loses to a flush.

STRAIGHT FLUSH: A five-card poker hand which contains both a straight and a flush simultaneously. Example:

It beats everything but a royal flush, which by definition really is the highest ranking straight flush.

JACK STRAUS: Won the Binion World Series of Poker in 1982.

STREET: Used to define the stage of a hand, usually in seven-stud. Sixth street is the betting round after the sixth card has been dealt; fourth street, the round after the fourth card, etc.

STRING BET: An illegal wager in which a player puts in some chips, then goes back to his or her stacks to get some more.

Usually, the rule is you must declare your bet or raise verbally if you intend to return to your stacks for more chips.

SUIT: A marking on a card other than its rank. There are four different suits (13 cards of each in a full deck): clubs, diamonds, hearts and spades.

TELL: A mannerism which allows you to determine, through observation of behavior, the kind of hand an opponent has.

THREE OF A KIND: A poker hand containing three cards of the same rank, such as 4-4-4. Beats two pair and loses to a straight.

TIGHT: Conservative play.

TURN: The fourth card on the board in hold 'em.

TWO PAIR: A poker hand consisting of two individual pair, such as:

or:

Ranks above one pair and below three of a kind.

STU UNGAR: Won the Binion World Series of Poker back to back in 1980 and 1981.

WILD CARD: A card that can be construed as anything you want it to be. For instance, if you were playing in a non-standard game where deuces were wild, then 8-8-7-7-2 would be a full house, since you would use the deuce as an eight.

ERNESTINE ZUERCHER: Did not win the Binion World Series of Poker. No woman ever has.

KEEPING YOUR GAMING
KNOWLEDGE CURRENT

Since February of 1977, readers of *Gambling Times* magazine have profited immensely. They have done so by using the information they have read each month. If that sounds like a simple solution to winnning more and losing less, well it is! Readers look to Gambling Times for that very specific reason. And it delivers.

Gambling Times is totally dedicated to showing readers how to win more money in every form of legalized gambling. How much you're going to win depends on many factors, but it's going to be considerably more than the cost of a subscription.

WINNING AND MONEY

Winning, that's what Gambling Times is all about. And money, that's what Gambling Times is all about. Because winning and money go hand in hand.

Here's what the late Vince Lombardi, the famous football coach of the Green Bay Packers, had to say about winning:

> It's not a sometime thing. Winning is a habit. There is no room for second place. There is only one place in my game and that is first place. I have finished second twice in my time at Green Bay and I don't ever want to finish second again. The objective is to win—fairly, squarely, decently, by the rules—but to win. To beat the other guy. Maybe that sounds hard or cruel. I don't think it is. It is, and has always been, an American zeal to be first in anything we do, and to win, and to win and to win.

Lombardi firmly believed that being a winner is "man's finest hour." Gambling Times believes it is too, while being a loser is depressing, ego-deflating, expensive and usually very lonely. "Everybody loves a winner" may be a cliche, but it's true. Winners command respect and are greatly admired. Winners are also very popular and have an abundance of friends. You may have seen a winner in a casino, with a bevy of girls surrounding him . . . or remember one who could get just about any girl he wanted.

Some of the greatest gamblers in the world also have strong views on what winning is all about. Here's what two of them have to say on the subject:

> To be a winner, a man has to feel good about himself and know he has some kind of advantage going in. I never made bets on even chances. Smart is better than lucky. "Titanic" Thompson

> When it comes to winnin', I got me a one-track mind. You gotta want to win more than anything else. And you gotta have confidence. You can't pretend to have it. That's no good. You gotta have it. You gotta know. Guessers are losers. Gamblin's just as simple as that. Johnny Moss

Gambling Times will bring you the knowledge you need to come home a winner and come home in the money. For it is knowledge, the kind of knowledge you'll get in its pages, that separates winners from losers. It's winning and money that *Gambling Times* offers you. *Gambling Times* will be your working manual to winning wealth.

The current distribution of this magazine is limited to selected newsstands in selected cities. Additionally, at newsstands where it is available, it's being snapped up, as soon as it's displayed, by gamblers who know a sure bet when they see one.

So if you're serious about winning, you're best off subscribing to *Gambling Times*. Then you can always count on its being there, conveniently delivered to your mailbox—and what's more, it will be there one to two weeks before it appears on the newsstands. You'll be among the first to receive the current issue as soon as it comes off the presses and being first is the way to be a winner.

Having every monthly issue of *Gambling Times* will enable you to build an "Encyclopedia of Gambling," since the contents of this magazine are full of sound advice that will be as good in five or ten years as it is now.

As you can see, a subscription to *Gambling Times* is your best bet for a future of knowledgeable gambling. It's your ticket to WINNING and MONEY.

FOUR NEW WAYS TO GET 12 WINNING ISSUES OF GAMBLING TIMES FREE ...

Every month over 250,000 readers trust *Gambling Times* to introduce powerful new winning strategies and systems. Using proven scientific methods, the world's leading experts show you how to win big money in the complex field of gambling.

Gambling Times has shown how progressive slot machines can be beat. Readers have discovered important new edges in blackjack. They've been shown how to know for sure when an opponent is bluffing at poker. *Gambling Times* has also spelled out winning methods for football, baseball and basketball. They've published profound new ways of beating the horses. Their team of experts will uncover information in the months ahead that's certain to be worth thousands of dollars to you.

In fact, the features are so revolutionary that they must take special precautions to make sure *Gambling Times* readers learn these secrets long before anyone else. So how much is *Gambling Times* worth to you? Well ...

NOW GAMBLING TIMES CAN BE BETTER THAN FREE!

Here's how: This **BONUS** package comes **AUTOMATICALLY TO YOU WHEN YOU SUBSCRIBE** ... or goes to a friend if you give a gift subscription.

(1) **POKER BONUS** at the **STARDUST** cardroom in Las Vegas. Play poker at the **STARDUST** and receive a free dinner buffet and comps to the Lido de Paris show for you and a guest. Value exceeds $40 excluding gratuities.

(2) **FREE SPORTS BET. CHURCHILL DOWNS SPORTS BOOK** in Las

Vegas will let you make one wager up to $300 with no "vigorish." This means instead of laying the usual 11-to-1 odds, you can actually bet even up! You can easily save $30 here.

(3) **PAYOFF BIGGER THAN THE TRACK. LEROY'S RACE BOOK** in Las Vegas will add 10% to your payoff (up to $30 extra) on a special bet. Just pick the horse and the race of your choice anywhere in America. For the first time in history, you can win more than the track pays.

(4) **OUTSTANDING ROOM DISCOUNTS** available only to *Gambling Times* subscribers. Check in at the **SANDS** in Atlantic City, the **STARDUST** in Las Vegas, or the **CONDADO** Inn & Casino in San Juan, Puerto Rico. Stay for 3 days and 2 nights and you'll save $29 off their normal low rates.

THAT'S A SAVING GREATER THAN THE ENTIRE COST OF YOUR SUBSCRIPTION.

USE ALL FOUR CERTIFICATES (VALID FOR ONE YEAR) ... GET GAMBLING TIMES FREE ... AND YOU'LL PUT $93 IN YOUR POCKET!

To begin your delivery of *Gambling Times* magazine at once, enclose a payment of $36.00 by check or money order (U.S. currency), MasterCard or Visa. Add $5.00 per year for postage outside the United States.

Send payment to:

GAMBLING TIMES MAGAZINE 1018 N. Cole Avenue,
Hollywood, California 90038

GAMBLING TIMES MONEY BACK GUARANTEE

If at any time you decide Gambling Times is not for you, you will receive a full refund on all unmailed copies. You are under no obligation and may keep the bonus as a gift.

OTHER VALUABLE SOURCES OF KNOWLEDGE AVAILABLE THROUGH GAMBLING TIMES

Here are some additional sources you can turn to for worthwhile gambling information:

Poker Player. Published every other week, this Gambling Times newspaper features the best writers and theorists on the poker scene today. You will learn all aspects of poker, from odds to psychology, as well as how to play in no-limit competition and in tournaments. Yearly subscriptions (26 issues) are $20.

Super/System. A Course in Power Poker By Doyle Brunson. The bible for poker players. This book contains contributions from poker's leading professionals, including Bobby Baldwin, Mike Caro and David Sklansky. An encyclopedia of more than 600 pages of detailed strategy for every form of poker.
Hardbound. $50.00 plus $3.00 shipping.

The Experts Blackjack Newsletter. This newsletter has all the top blackjack experts working just for you. Features answers, strategies and insights that were never before possible. Subscriptions for 12 consecutive issues are $60, $50 for *Gambling Times* subscribers. To order any of these publications, send your check or money order to: Gambling Times, 1018 N. Cole Avenue, Hollywood CA 90038.

OTHER BOOKS AVAILABLE

If you can't find the following books at your local bookstore, they may be ordered directly from Gambling Times, 1018 N. Cole Hollywood CA 90038. Information on how to order follows these listings.

POKER BOOKS

ACCORDING TO DOYLE. By Doyle Brunson. Acknowledged by most people as the world's best all-around poker player, twice World Champion Doyle Brunson brings you his homespun wisdom from over 30 years as a professional poker player. This book will not only show you how to win at poker, it will give you valuable insights into how to better handle that poker game called life.
Paperback. ISBN 0-89746-003-0. **$6.95**

CARO ON GAMBLING. By Mike Caro. The world's leading poker writer covers all the aspects of gambling from his regular columns in *Gambling Times* magazine and *Poker Player* newspaper. Discussing odds and probablilities, bluffing and raising, psychology and character, this book will bring to light valuable concepts that can be turned into instant profits in home games as well in the poker palaces of the West. Paperback. ISBN 0-89746-029-4. **$6.95**

MIKE CARO'S BOOK OF TELLS. The photographic body language of poker. By Mike Caro. 179 photos with text showing when a player is bluffing, when he's got the winning hand—and WHY. Even the greatest gamblers have some giveaway behavior. For the first time in print, one of the world's top poker players reveals how he virtually can read minds because nearly every player has a "tell." Seal the leaks in your poker game and empty your opponent's chip tray. Hardbound. ISBN 0-914314-04-1. **$20.00**

FREE MONEY. How to Win in the Cardrooms of California. By Michael Wiesenberg. Computer expert and poker writer *par excellence*, the author delivers critical knowledge to those who play in the poker rooms of the western states. Wiesenberg gives you the precise meaning of the rules, mathematical odds and strategies that work for either private or public games.
Paperback. ISBN 0-89746-027-8. **$8.95**

HOW TO WIN AT POKER TOURNAMENTS. By Tom McEvoy with Roy West. Tom McEvoy has played in more poker tournaments than anyone in the world. He has finished in the money in over $100, captured first place more than 60 times and won the 1983 World Series of Poker. McEvoy shows you the concepts and strategies needed to place in the money at poker tournaments. All you need is an understanding of poker. Paper. ISBN 0-89746-055-3. **$9.95**

NEW POKER GAMES. By Mike Caro. Inside this book are ten tested, balanced and proven new forms of poker. All were personally analyzed by "Mad Genius" Mike Caro. Some of these games are Caro's own creations while others were chosen from among the entries to his worldwide New Poker Games contest in *Gambling Times* magazine. Paperback. ISBN 0-89746-040-5. **$5.95**

THE RAILBIRD. By Rex Jones. The ultimate kibitzer, the man who watches from the rail in the poker room, has unique insights into the character and performance of all poker players. From this vantage point, Rex Jones, Ph.D., blends his lifetime of poker playing and watching. The result is a delightful book with exceptional values for those who want to avoid the fatal errors of bad players and capitalize upon the qualities that make outstanding poker players.
Paperback. ISBN 0-89746-028-6. **$6.95**

TALES OUT OUT OF TULSA. By Bobby Baldwin. Oklahoma born Bobby Baldwin, the youngest player to ever win the World Championship of Poker, is considered to be among the top five poker players in the world. Known affectionately as "The Owl," this brilliant poker genius rings the benefits of his experience to the pages of this book. It's sure to stop the leaks in your poker game, put you ahead of your opponents in the next game you play.
Paperback. ISBN 0-89746-006-5. **$6.95**

WINS, PLACES AND PROS. By Tex Sheahan. With more than 50 years of experience as a professional poker player and cardroom manager/tournament director, Sheahan reveals the secrets that separate the men from the boys at a poker table. Covers poker events, playing experiences, and players who are masters of the game. Paperback. ISBN 0-89746-008-1 **$6.95**

BEGINNERS GUIDE TO WINNING BLACKJACK. By Stanley Roberts. The world's leading blackjack writer shows beginners to the game how to obtain an instant advantage through the simplest of techniques. Covering basic strategy for all major casino areas from Las Vegas to the Bahamas, Atlantic City and Reno/Tahoe. Roberts provides a simple system to immediately know when the remaining cards favor the player. The entire method can be learned in less than two hours and taken to the casinos to produce sure profits.
Paperback. ISBN 0-89746-014-6. **$10.00**

GAMBLING TIMES GUIDE TO BLACKJACK. By Stanley Roberts with Edward O. Thorp, Ken Uston, Lance Humble, Arnold Snyder, Julian Braun, D. Howard Mitchell, Jerry Patterson and other experts in this field. The top blackjack authorities have been brought together for the first time to bring the reader the ins and outs of the game of blackjack. All aspects of the game are discussed. Winning techniques are presented for beginners and casual players.
Paperback. ISBN 0-89746-015-4. **$5.95**

MILLION DOLLAR BLACKJACK. By Ken Uston. Every blackjack enthusiast or gaming traveler who fancies himself a "21" player can improve his game with this explosive bestseller. Ken Uston shows you how he and his team won over $4,000,000 at blackjack. Now, for the first time, you can find out how he did it and how his system can help you. Includes playing and betting strategies, winning secrets, protection from cheaters. Uston's Advanced Point

Count System, and a glossary of inside terms used by professionals.

Paperback. ISBN 0-89746-068-5. **$14.95**

WINNING BLACKJACK. By Stanley Roberts. This is the simplest, most accurate system ever devised. The average person takes about eight hours both to read the system completely and master it. It does not require a photographic memory. All you really have to do is pay attention to the game. Businessmen and housewives alike report consistent winnings of up to $500 a day when using Roberts' system. This manual is complete in every way. It not only tells you how to play, it also tells you where to play, how much to bet and some very important tips about the art of casino play. There is a special section or beating multi-deck games and everything you need to know about blackjack in Las Vegas, Reno, Tahoe, Atlantic City and a host of other casino resorts around the world. This book has the power to completely transform your life! Winning Blackjack is large, 8-1/2x11", and includes pull-apart flashcards printed on card stock.

ISBN 0-914314-00-9. **$95.00**

CASINO GAMES

GAMBLING TIMES GUIDE TO CASINO GAMES. By Len Miller. The co-founder and editor of *Gambling Times* magazine vividly describes the casino games and explains their rules and betting procedures. This easy-to-follow guide covers blackjack, craps, roulette, keno, video machines, progressive slots and more. After reading this book, you'll play like a pro!

Paper. ISBN 0-89746-017-0. **$5.95**

GAMBLING TIMES GUIDE TO CRAPS. By N. B. Winkless, Jr. The ultimate craps book for beginners and experts alike. A chapter is devoted to a computer program that will let you test your system against the house. Text shows you which bets to avoid and tells you the difference between craps in Nevada and other gaming resort areas. Glossary of terms. Directory of dealer schools. Paperback. ISBN 0-89746-013-8. **$5.95**

BOOKS ON SYSTEMS. Gambling Times' library of gambling facts contained so much material that six system books had to be published. There is no duplicated material. In all there are 72 systems covering almost any type of gaming you can imagine.

GAMBLING TIMES GUIDE TO SYSTEMS THAT WIN. For those who want to broaden their gambling knowledge, this two volume set offers complete gambling systems used by the experts. Learn their strategies and how to incorporate them into your gambling style.

Volume I. Covers 12 systems that win for roulette, craps, backgammon, slot machines, horse racing, baseball, basketball and football.

Paperback. ISBN 0-89746-034-0. **$5.95**

Volume II. Features 12 more systems that win, covering horse racing, craps, blackjack, slot machines, jai alai and baseball.

Paperback. ISBN 0-89746-035-9. **$5.95**

GAMBLING TIMES GUIDE TO WINNING SYSTEMS. For those who take their gambling seriously. Gambling Times presents a two-volume set of proven winning systems. Learn how the experts beat the house edge and become consistent winners.

Volume I. Contains 12 complete strategies for casino games and sports wagering including: baccarat, blackjack, keno, basketball and harness handicapping.

Paperback. ISBN 0-89746-032-4. **$5.95**

Volume II. Features 12 more winning systems covering poker bluffing, pitching analysis, greyhound handicapping and roulette.

Paperback. ISBN 0-89746-033-2. **$5.95**

GAMBLING TIMES GUIDE TO WINNING SYSTEMS AND METHODS. This two volume collection of winning strategies by some of the nations leading experts on gambling will help you in your quest to beat the percentages.

Volume I. Includes several chapters on blackjack, as well as methods for beating baseball, basketball, hockey, steeplechase and grass racing.

Paperback. ISBN 0-89746-036-7. **$5.95**

Volume II. This volume contains an analysis of keno and video poker, as well as systems for success in sports betting and horse racing.

Paperback. ISBN 0-89746-037-5. **$5.95.**

GAMBLING TIMES QUIZ BOOK. By Mike Caro. Learn while testing your knowledge. Caro's book includes questions and answers on the concepts and information published in previous issues of *Gambling Times* magazine. Covers only established fact, not personal opinion.

Paperback. ISBN 0-89746-031-6. **$5.95**

THE MATHEMATICS OF GAMBLING. By Dr. Edward O. Thorp. The "Albert Einstein of gambling" presents his second book on the subject. His first book, *Beat the Dealer*, set the gambling world on its heels and struck fear into the cold-blooded hearts of Las Vegas casino owners in 1962. Now, more than twenty years later, Dr. Thorp again challenges the odds by bringing out a simple to understand version of more than thirty years of exploring all aspects of what separates winners from losers ... knowing the real meaning of the parameters of the games.   Paperback. ISBN 0-89746-019-7. **$7.95**

P$YCHING OUT VEGAS. By Marvin Karlins, Ph.D. The dream merchants who build and operate gaming resorts subtly work on the casino patron to direct his attention, control his actions and turn his pockets inside out. Their techniques are revealed by a noted psychologist who shows how to successfully control your behavior and turn a losing attitude into a lifetime winning streak.

Hardbound. ISBN 0-914314-03-3. **$12.00**

WINNING BY COMPUTER. By Donald Sullivan. The wonders of computer technology are harnessed for the gambler. Dr. Sullivan explains how to figure the odds and identify key factors in all forms of race and sports handicapping.   Paperback. ISBN 0-89746-018-9. **$5.95**

SPORTS BETTING BOOKS

FAST TRACK TO THOROUGHBRED PROFITS. By Mark Cramer. A unique approach to selecting winners by distinguishing between valuable and commonplace information. Results: higher average payoffs and profits. How to spot signs of improvement and when to cash in.ISBN 0-89746-025-1. **$6.95**

GAMBLING TIMES GUIDE TO BASKETBALL HANDICAPPING. By Barbara Nathan. The definitive guide to basketball betting. Expert sports handicapper Barbara Nathan provides handicapping knowledge, insight coverage, and step-by-step guidance for money management. Advantages and disadvantages of relying on sports services covered. Paper. ISBN 0-89746-023-5. **$5.95**

GAMBLING TIMES GUIDE TO FOOTBALL HANDICAPPING. By Bob McCune. Starting with the novice's approach to handicapping football and winding up with some of the more sophisticated team selection techniques in the sports handicapping realm. How to forecast the final scores of most major national football games.   Paperback. ISBN 0-89746-022-7. **$5.95**

GAMBLING TIMES GUIDE TO GREYHOUND RACING. By William E. McBride. Begins with a brief overview detailing the origins of greyhound racing and parimutuel betting, and explains track environment, betting procedures, and handicapping methods. Directory of various greyhound organizations and books. Section on famous dogs and personalities in the world of greyhound racing.   Paperback. ISBN 0-89746-007-3. **$5.95**

GAMBLING TIMES GUIDE TO HARNESS RACING. By Kusyshyn, Stanley and Dragich. Canada's top harness handicapping authorities present their inside approach to analyzing and selecting winners. Factors from the type of sulky, workouts, drivers' ratings, speed, pace, etc. Presented in simple terms for novices or experienced racegoers. Paper. ISBN 0-89746-002-2. **$5.95.**

GAMBLING TIMES GUIDE TO JAI ALAI. By William R. Keevers. The most comprehensive book on jai alai available. An informative journey from the ancient beginnings of the came to its current popularity. Easy-to-understand guide shows you the fine points of the game, how to improve your betting percentage, and where to find frontons. Paper. ISBN 0-89746-010-3. **$5.95**

GAMBLING TIMES GUIDE TO THOROUGHBRED RACING. By R. G. Denis. Informative description of the thoroughbred parimutuel activity by an experienced racing authority. Activities at the track and available information are blended skillfully in this guide to selecting winners that pay off in big-ticket returns.   Paperback. ISBN 0-89746-005-7. **$5.95**

ORDERING INFORMATION
Available at bookstores everywhere or order directly from:

Gambling Times 1018 N. Cole Ave. Hollywood CA 90038

For orders by mail please add shipping and handling charges as follows: Paperback books; $1.50 U.S., $2.00 Canada or Mexico, $4.00 foreign, per book. Hardbound books add $1.50 surcharge per book.